FINALIST
Best Spirituality Book
BOOKS FOR A BETTER LIFE AWARD, 2005

∽

"Valuable addition to the literature on mourning and bereavement."
—*Publishers Weekly,* starred review

∽

"The author writes a beautifully moving salve for the grief
and loss we all experience."
—*Cleveland Plain Dealer*

∽

"Levine has definitely taken up an important subject."
—*Shambhala Sun*

∽

"Levine attends to both body and soul in this beautifully written
meditation on recovering from grief."
—*Utne*

∽

"Your heart and soul can be made whole again, be rejuvenated, and best
of all, you can now overcome sorrow. All this is thanks to the gentle,
insightful, user-friendly wisdom of my friend, Steven Levine."
—Mark Victor Hansen, cocreator, #1 *New York Times* best-selling series
Chicken Soup for the Soul®; coauthor, *The One Minute Millionaire*

UNATTENDED SORROW

Recovering from Loss
and Reviving the Heart

STEPHEN LEVINE

RODALE

© 2005 by Stephen Levine
Cover photographs © Gunnar Smoliansky/Photonica (bench)
and Erin Hogan/Getty Images (flower)

Printed in the United States of America
Rodale Inc. makes every effort to use acid-free ♾, recycled paper ♻.

Book design by Christopher Rhoads

Library of Congress Cataloging-in-Publication Data

Levine, Stephen, date.
    Unattended sorrow : recovering from loss and reviving the heart / Stephen Levine.
        p.   cm.
    ISBN-13 978–1–59486–065–2 hardcover
    ISBN-10 1–59486–065–3 hardcover
    ISBN-13 978–1–59486–381–3 paperback
    ISBN-10 1–59486–381–4 paperback
    1. Grief.   2. Loss (Psychology)   I. Title.
BF575.G7L493   2005
155.9'37—dc22   2004024116

Distributed to the trade by Holtzbrinck Publishers

2 4 6 8 10 9 7 5 3 1 hardcover
2 4 6 8 10 9 7 5 3 1 paperback

LIVE YOUR WHOLE LIFE™

We inspire and enable people to improve their lives and the world around them

For more of our products visit **rodalestore.com** or call 800-848-4735

This book is dedicated to my wife and spiritual partner, Ondrea, who has been by my side for every step of the learning process: and for the love of whom, when I contemplate its loss, attunes me to the tragedy that so many we have served experienced.

And I would additionally like to dedicate this book to my dear friend Elisabeth Kübler-Ross, who, in one of those "cosmic coincidences" in which she so delighted, died within hours of the completion of this book, the last in a series of books on the subject she initiated me into thirty years ago. We meet a few people along the way that change our lives; may all who read this find what I found in Elisabeth.

CONTENTS

CONTENTS

CONTENTS

PREFACE

THIS BOOK BEGAN AS A THIRTY-TWO-PAGE PAMPHLET
MEANT TO BE DISTRIBUTED BY THE RED CROSS to the wives of
the firemen killed in the fall of the Twin Towers. It was completed two
weeks after the deaths, but because the Red Cross said they were already overwhelmed with goodwilled materials, they doubted the
booklet would get to those I wished. So I undertook to extend that
booklet into a book, incorporating the difficulties that may lie ahead
for them and for us all, with an encouragement that those grieved
thoughts, which may certainly remain, find your heart in which to come
to rest.

UNATTENDED SORROW

INTRODUCTION

FROM MY TWENTY-FIVE YEARS WORKING WITH THE IMME-
DIACY OF GRIEF in and around the deathbed, it gradually became evident how previous, unresolved loss seemed to intensify the blow of
imminent death. My wife, Ondrea, and I have been called upon over
the years to extend our grief work to concentration camp survivors and
their children, as well as Vietnam War veterans and eventually the victims of sexual abuse. We found that the long-range impact of grief became painfully evident in almost every area of their lives. We saw, too,
how, to a lesser degree, the unresolved (unintegrated) loss of a loved
one, even years before, had the same numbing effect. Over the years it
became increasingly obvious that grief and the spirit were the two

common denominators, the two underlying characteristics of all people, the ever-present potential for hell or heaven at any moment.

For those unable to make peace with their pain, there was a gradual diminishment of their life force. It became obvious that it was not just the most recent griefs that underlay their intermittent depression and dysfunction but the imprint of losses long past—yet still painfully present.

We came to see that what had come to be called post-traumatic distress disorder had causes that accumulated daily. The aftereffects of violence—added to by each abuse and each most recent war—is only part of what is profoundly ailing us.

The long-range impact of unresolved sorrow flows along a hidden spectrum. At one end are the deaths and innumerable unacknowledged losses that cause the scarring and callusing that numb our surface: they are the obstacles to the heart. Spanning these long-unattended sorrows, which gradually close us down, are the slowly accumulating burdens of disappointment and disillusionment, the loss of trust and confidence that follows the increasingly less satisfactory arch of our lives—until finally, at the far end of the spectrum we are so mired in lost hope that we are barely able to find ourselves.

The work throughout this book does not purport to stop grief from arising, but only to help process the grief in whatever way it manifests, before it affects consciousness from a place well below the level of our awareness, and before producing such emotions as anxiety or fear or anger that arise when we don't know why we feel the way we do.

1

UNATTENDED SORROW

DURING OUR YEARS OF WORKING WITH PEOPLE CON-FRONTING LOSSES, from a death earlier that day or one chronically embedded from decades before, my wife, Ondrea, and I were often moved by how many asked if they were grieving "correctly."

How merciless we can be with ourselves.

Nothing is more natural than grief, no emotion more common to our daily experience. It's an innate response to loss in a world where everything is impermanent. We don't know what to do with our pain, and we never have. We have been told to bury our feelings, to keep a stiff upper lip, to "get over it and get on with our lives" as though loss were not an inevitable part of life. As a result, our sorrow goes unattended and manifests itself in many unexpected ways.

It weakens the body and compartmentalizes the mind. We become one part love and three parts fear, two parts trust and five parts doubt. We are more greed than generosity, part ignorance and part wisdom. Some doors are locked and some flung wide open, each part discrete from the rest, no whole person to be found.

Unattended sorrow disturbs sleep and infects our dreams; unable to find our way "home" all night, we feel lost all day. Nightly conflicts wear through our days. When sorrows are caught in the mind-net, lacking alternatives, such thoughts and feelings repeatedly arise. Caught in cycles of self-condemnation, our sorrow saps our energy with fantasies and reveries.

It inhibits intuition. We come to trust ourselves less. We cannot "feel" the world around us as we once did, so we experience ourselves as "a bit unplugged." We feel ourselves a bit withdrawn, a little dead on our peripheries, a bit numb at the fingertips, our listless tongue lying sideways like a sunken ship on the floor of the mouth. This quality of grief can slow our creativity and "dumb us down" a bit.

Sorrow often makes a relationship a place to hide instead of an opportunity to open. It's the compulsive busying of our lives, our fear that if we slow down for just a minute we may be overtaken by sorrow or hear too much of what lies beneath the mind-chatter—the loneliness, and the need for denial just to feel sane.

Unresolved grief is like a low-grade fever. It flows in peaks and valleys. Sometimes it spikes into almost overwhelmingly afflictive emotions; at other times it lies almost dormant, nearly comatose, just beneath the surface, until a shadow crosses the heart and releases it.

It is not uncommon for those with unattended sorrow to lean toward addictions of all sorts, from food or drugs to dangerous behavior and other forms of self-mutilation. Unattended sorrow affects our appetite, whether in the form of overeating or self-starvation. Distressed by continuing uncertainty, we swallow everything that comes close, and feel guilty that we are not somehow different—less pained, less hungry, less depressed—than we are. And shame, like a dishonest lover, calls to us from the shadows and slows us yet more . . . woefully reaffirming our guilt. As one person said, "I eat too much because I eat too much." Alcoholics also voice that same rationalization, rather than noting beneath their smoldering suffering that they drink because they feel empty (psychologically empty, a feeling of rootless vacuity) or conversely because they feel too full (psychological heaviness, a deadness of the spirit).

Sorrows that are lost in the shadows can either numb our sexuality or turn it frantic. We become so numb we cannot touch or be touched, cannot feel or be felt, cannot love or be loved. Or, from that insensitivity, we become sexually destructive to ourselves or someone else.

The pain has been there for as long as we can remember, so familiar that we barely recognize it until the impact of unmistakable loss stares back at us.

Unattended sorrow narrows the path of our lives. We endure so many forms of loss in the unpredictable course of a lifetime. There are so many circumstances that befall us that cause us to lose heart. And we are often at a loss to express the depth of those feelings.

For many people, it is not only the loss of a loved one through death that causes them to lose confidence in what lies ahead but a long-fading trust in life itself; the residue of rejections and abandonments; of the humiliations of illness, old age, and death; of the loss of certainty; the disillusionment of expectations. It's the reservoir of lost promise, of lost faith, and of the gradually decreasing appreciation for life.

Our unattended sorrow contains everything we've lost and all we'll never have. Our confidence that we could make life happen as we wished, our belief in unquestioned expectations, is wounded. Our uncertainty filters every perception. We live our life as an afterthought.

Our traumas, great and small, seemingly irreducible or ever hidden, may challenge our faith in life and leave us conflicted by many of life's desires and our deeper longings that go unrecognized and unsatisfied.

Trying to protect ourselves from pain limits us and pushes away all that we love, leaving us feeling isolated. But if we gently explore layer after layer of our clinging to our pain, we beckon love to accompany us on the path to healing. Ironically, we are not alone in our feelings of isolation. We are a part of the worldwide community of loss. If sequestered pain made a sound, the atmosphere would be humming all the time. We close around our pain by refusing it mercy, by resisting the softening and letting go that might give it a little more space to breathe.

～

If we listen for unattended sorrow as we might for a cry from a crib in the next room, we can hear it calling to us to have mercy on ourselves and move forward with a heartful examination of our lingering disappointment and distress, instead of turning our back on it. When we turn away from our sorrow, we intensify our pain and close off parts of ourselves.

One of the great barriers to becoming whole once again is doubt. Because we are powerless against our pain, we think we are stuck where we are and cannot move in any direction. But it is the kind investigation into the acceptance of that powerlessness that can offer the hope. Investigating our feelings of powerlessness increasingly empowers us to reenter those parts of ourselves long since abandoned to helplessness and hopelessness. Rather than deflecting unpleasant feelings or memories, we explore the possibilities of the heart one breath at a time.

If we allow it to, an unexpected mercy and a little recognized level of awareness may exhume us from our suffering. Naturally, attending to this sorrow isn't going to make it all vanish. But it does begin to unearth the heart that has room for it all, not leaving these feelings buried in an unmarked grave.

Tapping the resources of the heart—the power to forgive, the strength to love, the trust to look deeper into what limits us, and the path toward peace—allows us to settle unfinished business, to tie the loose ends of relationships, the unforgiven and unforgiving detritus that is carried from relationship to relationship, from job to job, from friend to friend, or from thought to thought. As forgiveness decomposes the armoring over our heart, we release the grief that's been held hard in the body: releasing, moment to moment, the muscle shield that's tightened for self-protection across the abdomen, softening breath after breath to sorrow after sorrow. When we soften layer after layer of the armoring over the heart, we open to the possibility of a new life and offer to ourselves gifts greater than those of the Magi, heralding the continuation of our birth.

Part of this process of liberating the heart is incorporated in daylong experiments in healing: days devoted to embracing loss with a liberating awareness that sees clearly into it; days of fearlessness, of taking birth anew, of learning once again how to walk and breathe and find "the still small voice within"; and days devoted to opening into the heart of pain. The pages of this book will guide you in how to begin these processes. When we reenter the body and mind through the heart—via a developing mindfulness and forgiveness, loving kindness and gratitude, silence and prayer—we add day after day to a life of love. When we turn to our innate wisdom for the harmony of mind and gut, we heal the entrance to the heart as it seeks to beat in rhythm with the world.

2

EVERY DAY WE LOSE SOMETHING

LOSS IS THE ABSENCE OF SOMETHING WE WERE ONCE ATTACHED TO. Grief is the rope burns left behind, when that which is held is pulled beyond our grasp. I know very few people who are not grieving at some level. Feelings of loss don't go away; they go deeper. When we lose or never exercise what we need or love, we call the hard contraction in the mind and body "suffering." This is our unattended sorrow.

I'm speaking not only of unexpected loss but the usual, everyday loss: the loss of dignity due to racial and religious prejudice, or the multitude of finely wrought cultural humiliations suffered by women, the aged, children, the infirm, and the less than "beautiful."

I'm speaking of an underlying sorrow in most people that encircles their heart and begs for merciful attention. It is the ungrieved losses of love betrayed, of trusts broken, of lies sent and received, of words spoken that can never be retrieved, and of the repeated bruises left by unkindness. It is the long-delayed grief of miscarriages and betrayals, lost opportunities, a thousand and one insults, and clutching misgivings that ricochet in the mind and instill restlessness and depression. It's the unfinished business, the self-healing yet to be undertaken, the apathy and angst that inform our lives.

We have given short shrift to so many of these losses, great and small, and allowed them to sink well below the level of our awareness. This gives these wounds the power to hold the reins on so much of our self-defeating, self-negating behavior.

Though our remnant sorrows may seem no more than a pain in the neck (sometimes quite literally), they are actually the basis for a considerable limitation on our personal freedom. It is a suffering that needs to be recognized as not solely the acute circumstance that finds us contracted in agony, as one may think of suffering, but also a chronic, underlying condition amassed from the losses, rejections, dissatisfactions, and disappointments of the past. It is to the wide swath of grief, acute and chronic, gross and subtle, that this book is addressed: from losses as seemingly trivial as old insults to those still as invasive as the past wounds of the suicide of a loved one, abandonment, or violence.

DIMENSIONS OF GRIEF

Acute grief is the immediacy of loss—the inconceivable tragedy. It can feel like a stabbing sensation in the body and mind. It slams shut the heart and leaves exposed only raw emotions. It leaves very little space for anything but the sorrow, anger, fear, and doubt that attend to it.

Acute grief is a thunderstorm, a monsoonal downpour, a sudden flood that submerges almost everything in its path. This was Darla's experience when her husband died suddenly in an automobile accident.

"At first it was as though I had been struck by lightning, as if everything was stripped away. The shock was like a terrible jolt to my heart.

"At first when he died, it was like a great opening tore through me. I didn't know what to do with my life. I came into the kitchen and didn't know which way to turn. Everything felt so unreal. It was like I was waiting to wake up. I could barely hang on."

In acute grief, our difficulty finishing business with a departed loved one, as painful as it can be, may create repeated images of previous loss; the loss of one's mother, for instance, can cause us to recall in some detail other losses in the family. Or a radio news flash about an accident on the turnpike might bring the mind back to the bloody emergency room and the body to be identified. And yet as each fresh loss recapitulates all loss, it may inundate the mind with all the unfinished business of life. The grief of unacknowledged, seemingly irrational—but nonetheless painful—feelings of abandonment, anger, fear, and even unrecompensed love may persist in the resonance between one loss and all loss.

Jamal, who was reeling after the death of his partner, Peter, began to question whether he was grieving the acute loss of Peter or for all the people he'd ever lost. As he unsuccessfully wrestled with the inclination of acute grief to attach to all the pain and fear already residing in his mind from previous loss, numbed by an overload of feelings, he said,

"I feel like I'm drowning. I don't know how to live anymore. It seems all I do is put one foot in front of the other, just to get through it. It feels as though it's never going to end. And I think that's the most difficult because I don't know who I'm grieving for. Is it Peter? Is it all the others? Who is it?"

When acute grief is entangled by the loose ends of previous loss, the ensuing confusion can stymie the mind and leave the heart out in the cold. What odd creatures we are that when the heart aches most, calling us to most directly attend to its pain, we may be least likely to do so. Our mind is so full we have no refuge in our heart, which during this time would be the only safe harbor.

Chronic grief is this persistent ache in the heart—the phantom pain at the irreducible absence of a loved one or of ourselves. The initial acute grief of the loss of a loved one often resonates with the chronic grief that accumulates over the course of a lifetime. Chronic grief is the slowly receding waters and the damage revealed when the tsunami of acute grief subsides. It's the reservoirs caught in the depressions left by one unintegrated loss after another.

To oversimplify, there are at least two kinds of chronic grief. The first is the unresolved grief from earlier loss, the incomplete or interrupted process of finishing business by which we might sense our loved one more as a presence in the heart than one dislocated in thought. The second kind of chronic grief is our inherent, ordinary grief that results from unsatisfied desire, from the frequently unfulfilled ambitions and lost loves, and from the battering flow of impermanence in the world within and around us, which puts what we want at our fingertips, then pulls it away. It is a subtle nausea that undulates just beneath our ordinary, well-composed exterior.

It is not only the loose ends of recent traumas that are the cause of our grief, but those traumas long sequestered in our flesh and bones. The hurt burrows into the tissues of our body and the fiber of our mind and contracts around pain, turning it into suffering. The unwillingness to touch our pain with mercy, even with forgiveness, amplifies our discontent and throws our life out of tune.

The leap of faith necessary to cross the broken heart is yet to be taken. The history of loss that is still encoded in our senses warps each incoming perception and outgoing message. We construct labyrinthine defenses and a moat around our heart to allow some semblance of safety from our grief. Unattended sorrow gradually displaces the joy of youth and adds to the diminishment of trust and hope.

We grieve the deaths halfway around the world from famine, war, and spiritual poverty—losses that seem so distant, yet the sting of unattended sorrow's tears wells behind our eyes. It is a single grief that connects us, world-weary, to those everywhere who are barely surviving life. We grieve the loss of love and loved ones; experience fear, remorse, and the loss of trust in what may come next. And we grieve the tendency to mistake our pain for the truth, to think we deserve to suffer just because we are.

We keep so much of ourselves at a "safe distance" from the rest of our life that seldom do we directly experience the moment. And there's nothing in us that makes us feel quite so unsafe, so insecure, as trying to maintain that safety, that failing sense of control. It is the "normal human unhappiness," which Freud felt was the best that could be achieved by psychoanalysis. It sells us short.

I certainly do not mean to imply that what follows in these pages will cure all that ails you. But there are keys here to locked doors, lights for unlit hallways. These are maps to the center of our sorrow that can deliver us from deep forgetfulness and self-neglect. Maps that once pressed against the heart lead toward a life greater than what we might imagine is possible.

We are learning to live with the consequences of love. So we must bear loss as deeply as we cared. Throughout spiritual literature we are told that attachment creates pain, and here we are, trying to learn how to love more fully in the shadow of that very painful truth! But the irony is that without some level of attachment, *there could be no love.* As the Dalai Lama has said, "No attachment, no compassion."

It is the balancing act of a lifetime.

Attending to our sorrow, queasy with bewilderment at whom we might be without, we must first cultivate mercy for ourselves, which will gradually expand into compassion for other sentient beings. We send wishes for the well-being of all who, like ourselves, share this same pain at this same moment and who also wish only to be free. Using the mirror of compassionate mindfulness, we recognize our reflection amongst the throngs of sentient beings to whom the true heart, the healed heart, pledges service.

As the Buddha said, hard as it may be to embrace, "You can look the whole world over and never find anyone more deserving of love than yourself."

3

THE HEART
OF LOSS

THE LOSS OF A LOVED ONE OFTEN LEAVES BEHIND THE
LOOSE ENDS OF GRIEF.

We hate to be in pain, so we turn away as soon as we are able. Soon
the pain is submerged from view, yet it continues to affect our emotions
from well below the level of our awareness.

There is no magical cure for grief. In fact, for many people, grief includes a feeling of the loss of magic in one's life, a deep uncertainty that
we will ever be able to survive intact with this much pain. The hardness
in the belly personifies just how much we need to let go, and just how
much we long to take a free breath and let life back into the body.

But, just because underlying discomfort seems a common denominator, there still may be an alternative to living tentatively. Otherwise, there would be no easing of the "burden" and no chance of liberation. Our sorrow may go unattended because we feel helpless to do anything about it. Injured by the wayside, overwhelmed by a helplessness that leaves us feeling hopelessly victimized by life, we are lost between realms in what sometimes seems a very dark night of the soul.

I first heard about mindfulness practice during a soul-sad time in my life, and, though I was fearful that my sorrow might consume me, I was also doubtful that any spiritual inquiry would be of much help. Focusing inward, it seemed, just made me think more. I feared meditation might even be harmful to someone in a lot of pain or that it might be more trouble than it was worth. But my grief insisted. I had to make a deal with myself to give mindfulness practice a chance to kill me or cure me. Actually, in retrospect, I don't think it did either, but it certainly aided my heart to still be available under difficult circumstances.

⌒

Sometimes we feel helpless to defend ourselves against the cramping of the heart, even years after a loss. Our shoulders become heavy and our bellies sore, a dull ache defines our body, our necks stiffen, and our gait increasingly shortens.

Helplessness gives rise to our most noticeable griefs. It is the basis for a considerable amount of anger and aggression. In an attempt to over-come the feeling of having no control, the mind attempts to assert what-ever power it hopes will hide the fear and sense of profound aloneness. Aggression toward others and ourselves is akin to the muscle fatigue of swimming as hard as we can and still being dragged farther out to sea. The less we investigate our state of helplessness, the greater the poten-tial we have for self-destructive behavior. But once we open our hearts to our pain and to our hopelessness, we find that we are never truly helpless.

When we turn toward our pain instead of away from it, self-mercy enters those parts of ourselves we had closed off, withdrawn from, or abandoned to feelings of impotence. When it seems there is nowhere else to turn, when all our prayers and strategies seem to be of little avail, something deeper arises: a mercy that leads toward the heart.

To borrow an image from E. L. Doctorow, grief is like driving at night: though you can see only a few feet ahead of you, you can make the whole journey that way.

Without mercy (a quality of loving kindness that is the tender accep-tance of even those who might be otherwise unacceptable) as an alter-native to holding to our pain, we abandon those most painful memories within us to harsh judgment and merciless reflection. The teaching of mercy, a term sometimes used interchangeably with compassion, and the value of clarity is absolutely unmistakable in difficult situations as we learn to open into that which once closed us off.

Mercy is forgiveness or leniency. Sometimes it is even said that it means a boon or blessing—in this case, the boon of mindfulness and the blessing of loving kindness.

I'm not suggesting that our grief will completely go away, but rather that it can come to rest in the open heart and softening belly. Memories may always be bittersweet, but we may also find peace flickering at the edges of what once caused us agitation. Healing, then, becomes not the absence of pain but the increased ability to meet it with mercy instead of loathing. No one can wholly remove our pain. All we can do is increase the spaciousness of mind and heart in which it is allowed to decompress. Letting go is letting be.

As a result, we find ourselves exploring the capacity to slowly increase that space in which even great grief—the loss of a love, the loss of a child, the loss of innocence, the loss of faith—can be experienced. We find ourselves meeting helplessness with a simple kindness that confounds our addiction to critical self-judgment. We find ourselves more likely to meet others' confusion and helplessness openheartedly. We find ourselves with less need for others or ourselves to be different in order to be loved.

We find ourselves.

In order to balance our fear with our courage, we must trust our pain enough to explore it. Fear is our first unsuccessful attempt to protect ourselves from pain. The pretense of painlessness is the next. But it is the surrender of resistance that opens pain to healing. In order to open our hearts to our pain, we must be willing to experience it wholeheartedly.

There comes a point where it is more important to just let our heart break and get on with it than to keep trying to figure out why we are so often in pain or who's at fault and what sort of punishment they deserve. It takes a lot of work to get healed, to merge the heart and the disheartened. But even in the least observation, it becomes clear that no one needs any excuse for being in so much pain. Wherever there is expectation or broken hope, disappointment or loss, there is the stuff of Shakespearean malady.

Healing is entering, with mercy and awareness, into those areas of ourselves we have withdrawn from with fear and a sense of helplessness. Healing is reoccupying those parts of ourselves that we abandoned because of mental or physical pain. Healing is replacing our merciless reactions with a merciful response.

Without mercy, we don't have a chance. And that chance is the breadth of heart that is our birthright.

4

SOFTENING THE BELLY OF SORROW

WE HOLD OUR GRIEF HARD IN THE BELLY. We store fear and disappointment, anger and guilt in our gut. Our belly has become fossilized with a long resistance to life and to loss. Each withdrawal, each attempt to numb our grief, turns the belly to stone. Have mercy on this pain you have carried for so long, the pain that sometimes makes you want to jump out of your body.

Quite naturally, in the process of girding for self-protection, our belly guards old wounds and steels for the battle. Over the years, we have buried the ache of impermanence and the remnants of fear and helplessness there. A shield develops across our abdomen, which mirrors the armoring over our heart. As we soften around the sensations and gradually into them, they melt at the edge. It's not opposing the hardness but rather meeting it with soft mercy, *knowing that we cannot let go of anything we do not accept.* But sometimes, as much out of exhaustion as self-mercy, we momentarily let go of the rigidity that holds our suffering in place. Our belly softens for just a moment, and we get a glimpse beyond grief.

When we soften the fear-hardened belly, letting go of the tightness gives us space in which to process afflictive emotions. When we begin to soften to the knot of sensations that accompany a sense of loss in the belly, heart, and mind, there is a gradual release of pressure. As we soften to the fear, anger, and distrust that hardens us against life, we discover a lifetime's worth of grief in the belly. This is our unattended sorrow, from beyond which some inherent mercy calls upon us to release the heart.

As we soften the belly, letting go of trying to control the rise and fall of each breath but instead observing it as sensations come and go with each inhalation and exhalation, we begin to free level after level of holding. In the levels and levels of softening are levels and levels of letting go. Let old holdings begin to float in the new openness created by softening, as there arises a new willingness to heal, to go beyond our pain. As we begin to soften the belly, we unburden the body and mind of their automatic withdrawal from and walling-off of pain. As these burdens begin to lift, we find ourselves a bit lighter and the road ahead that much easier to travel; we're a bit more able to continue on with our lives.

"Going on with our lives," though it may seem somehow sacrilege, is in our own time the work we do to honor the life we share with all who have ever been born and will ever die. By opening into the possibilities of the heart, expanding the space that is able to absorb all that is let go of, we are able to find our own true compass of what is appropriate to our own healing and go mercifully on with our lives.

Marcus, a fellow who had spent a considerable amount of time in the military, approached Ondrea and me at a workshop, weeping for the fact that he had been taught his whole adult life to hold tight in his belly, to "have a fighting gut." He said that as he began to soften his belly, just as the tension began to loosen, "harder than hell, it snapped shut like a rat trap." He said in those momentary glimpses of softness, he sighed so deeply it made him cry.

Gradually, our attention settles into the abdomen and begins riding the rising and falling of the ocean of our breath. On the inhalation, the belly rises with the tide. On the exhalation, the tide goes out. A liberating awareness begins to settle in as we soften to the breath and to the distrust that hardens us to life. Let thoughts come and let thoughts go in a soft belly, without holding, and without resistance.

The healing practice is done by sitting quietly, closing your eyes and just letting your attention come into the sensations of the body. Feeling the body you sit in, you begin to bring your attention into the abdomen, feeling the belly rise and fall with each breath. And you begin to soften the abdominal muscles, letting go of whatever holding tightens your belly and maintains your suffering, softening the tissue all the way into the belly.

Make room for the breath as it breathes itself in soft belly, noticing how much grief there is in the form of resistance and an ache held deep in the belly. So much fear and armoring. Let it all float in soft belly, not hardening it to suffering, just letting it be in soft belly, in merciful belly.

Let go with each inhalation, softening the belly. Let go with each exhalation, making peace. Soften the belly to uncover the heart. Each exhalation lets out the pain. Make room for our life in soft belly.

Expectation, judgment, doubt, and all sorts of old griefs congregate in the belly. Softening allows them to disperse. Pains, fears, and doubts dissolve into the softness, the spaciousness of a merciful belly. Even the hardness floats in the softness. And there's nothing to change, we are just attending to ourselves; there is no urgency in soft belly.

There is room for our pain in soft belly. The spaciousness in the belly mirrors the opening of the heart.

When you open your eyes, maintaining this increased awareness, notice at what point the belly tightens once again. At what point does the sense of loss reassert itself and you feel a need to protect against further pain? At what point does the armoring reestablish its long presence?

Soften with the eyes wide open to the world, softening to the pain we all share and the legacy of healing exposed in our deepening softness.

Many people say they come back to softening the belly dozens of times a day. And it's a better day for it. Some begin the day with this exercise for fifteen minutes or more and notice how this softening in the body produces a deeply relieving letting go in the mind.

There are considerable gradations of our capacity to stay soft and work with things that we don't think we can. When we think we're not up to our grief, that's a form of grief. When we distrust ourselves and the process, our grief sometimes misinforms us about our capacity to work with it. When we soften to that grief, we find that even when we feel hopeless, we are not helpless.

Softening the belly won't perfect us, but it can set us free. It initiates a letting go, which frees the mind to open the heart.

We hold our unattended sorrow hostage in the belly, marbled in the muscle tissue with fear. Our resistance to life and our impatience with ourselves rigidifies the belly and excludes the possibilities of the heart. It makes shallow the breath. But softening the muscles, softening even the flesh, letting go of the age-old tension held there as if our life depended on it, invites the breath, invites life, deeper within.

When we come back again and again throughout the day to a soft belly, a sense of ease increases, which allows the quality of being loving to flow unimpeded, as natural as breathing.

Softening the belly demonstrates how self-mercy affects our reality.

In a soft belly, there is room to live and to grow, as our nature allows. Room to let go of the judgment that considers us somehow imperfect, room to send with each softening breath loving kindness into the grateful heart.

5

THE RESERVOIR
OF SORROW

REPEATED LOSS ACCUMULATES IN THE RESERVOIR OF
SORROW. It is the repository of all we have ever lost, all that died despite our love, all we ever hoped to be, all the disappointment and despair buried over a lifetime. Those places within ourselves that have
been dug away by loss, those parts lost, worn away, and excavated by
a gradually increasing helplessness and apathy, slowly begin to fill with
sorrow.

Unattended sorrow is a stone stuck in the throat from "swallowing
our grief," a boulder rolled into the entrance to the heart against our
resurrection. It is a great wounding of hope. We are afloat in unat-

tended sorrow, our head sometimes barely above the surface, struggling against the ever-changing undertow, at times from the long-deferred pain surrounding the death of a loved one, at other moments nearly pulled below the surface by our long absence from life.

It is said that in every loss there is an opportunity to uncover and heal the losses of a lifetime. The deeper the loss, the deeper the opportunity for healing. By opening to the little losses and the little deaths and the small sorrows, we make room for the greater griefs and the bigger losses, as we directly approach our life. The loose ends of grief float, a tangled web of sargasso on the reservoir of sorrow.

Consider Jim, who was long in a malaise, long past savoring his life, entangled in the web of sorrow. He said,

"I don't think I'm dealing with anything that has happened to me in the last forty years. My parents split up when I was ten. My younger brother died when I was seventeen. My sister died when I was five, and I think maybe I was supposed to be watching after her but looked away and she was hit by a car.

"I think, maybe, I have been so overwhelmed by it all that I can't feel anything. And I feel bad for not feeling worse. Sometimes I feel envy for the people who are going through their grief, their good days and bad days.

"I've even tried the prescribed idea of sending love into my pain, but it never really works because I can't find my love any more than I can find my pain. So I tried to conjure up some remembrance of love that might be applied. It was a memory of love as a warmness. And then it occurred to me that the love I couldn't find in me may be hidden inside my pain.

"I think I had to put my love away many years ago. And this pain is where I've put it. It's hiding somewhere inside my pain. It's pain-protected."

Sometimes, when we're adrift on the reservoir of sorrow in our own leaky little boat, we have to surrender our numbing pain to reach the shore, to make the pain the object of care instead of reinforcing resistance. Feeling the heart literally aching to be free, we begin to sense what it might be like to turn to ourselves, not with the fear and dread with which we usually approach pain, but with kindness.

The earth is sodden with grief, and we are picnicking on the slippery banks of loss. Most incredibly, even in our most abject grieving, not a single state of mind is new. Guilt, fear, anger, remorse, bewilderment, a sense of abandonment, confusion—none of it is new, and certainly not the isolation we have been all too familiar with for most of our lives. This isolation is the odd legacy of haphazard social individuation, of trying on all the masks of "a valued someone" and finding that most chafe, of losing our place in an interconnected universe, of wishing to come in from the cold.

In those periodic "ice ages," when fear and unattended sorrow eclipse

the spirit, there may be an insistence that the icy way, that nihilistic depression, is the only appropriate response—that a withdrawal from life
honors the dead. In those times, clogged with doubt, we may suffer
enormous uncertainty that unhinges the mind and ask ourselves, "Is
anything real?" When no mental construct of self or the world will suffice, turning toward the pain with whatever mercy is still available, we
find a deeper truth. We find at the base of the melting glacier a rivulet
running toward what Buddhist monks call the Ocean of Compassion.
When, as Thomas Merton says, "prayer has become impossible and the
heart has turned to stone," surrendering into the heart reveals the true
nature of prayer and the longing for wholeness.

As we emerge from the ice, the untapped potential of the heart is
called to the fore. Merciful awareness and compassionate intentions
warm the mind and body and bring us back to life. We let ourselves be
with our feelings as they arise, without scrambling for control over
them. Hell is resistance. If we can meet this moment in mercy, we increase the possibility, even the tendency, to meet the next moment in
mercy. But, if in this moment we deny our pain its due mercy "three
times before the dawn," then how will we roll the boulder from the
mouth of the cave? How will we clear the hindrances from the entrance
to our heart? How will we be able to take a single clear breath?

6

LOSS OF TRUST
IN LIFE

AS THE MYRIAD LOSSES OF A LIFETIME ACCUMULATE and deepen the reservoir of grief, it is sometimes difficult to see the other shore—or even trust that there *is* another shore.

One of the major inhibitors to the quality of trust is the shock to our system when it's struck by unforeseen loss. The more unexpected the wound, the longer it may take us to make peace with it.

One woman who lost her husband in the bombing of the Alfred R. Murrow Federal Building in Oklahoma City said afterward that her heart was like "that half-missing building."

Loss may come suddenly in the form of an unexpected diagnosis or gradually with the decrease in vigor from aging or the eclipse of vitality from illness. Or it can come as a slow deadening of the nerves and tightening of the heart by the family terrorism of physical, emotional, sexual, spousal, or child abuse.

To create a scale of trauma would be to oversimplify our feelings. A burglary, a mugging, the betrayal or abandonment by one to whom we are committed, a rape, or the death of a child can each shred our safety nets to increasing degrees.

For some people, loss comes in feeling victimized by a raging fire or an earthquake. For others, it's the recently notarized deceit of big businesses and the loss of savings and retirement benefits. If we're unable to count on our employment as our income disappears, we may feel like a pawn in a game others are playing. A feeling of helplessness breeds the anger that is flotsam on the reservoir of loss. The heart is clogged with fear and disappointment. In a world of incessant change, a feeling of great insecurity arises. Our life-account seems far overdrawn.

Some people mourn the absence of a loved one, some the loss of safety or of confidence in the uncertain course of our lives. We don't quite trust what might come next; it feels as though the ground beneath our feet must be tested with each step.

As we open to our unattended sorrow, the armoring and pain that distrust acquires layer by layer sometimes cause us to distance ourselves from our lives, to live outside our body. The armoring and the pain become so distinct, we think our heart will burst. Our healing can be so physically and mentally painful, yet so reaffirming of our ability to survive the worst of it. We even find the heart to gradually meet the mercilessness of others with mercy.

We are members of the community of impermanence. Uncontrollable change washes the past away behind us. Yet, harboring distrust limits our future. When we're threatened by the cold indifference that casts aside the old and the young, the sickest and the poorest, our fellow beasts and shared planet, a hopelessness arises that numbs trust.

And some people lose trust in the world soon after being born because of illness or abuse, or the incomplete emotional processing of a sibling's or parent's death that was silenced in the family. Some people lose trust from the ridicule of their peer group or the negligence of caretakers. Many people lose trust because of the moral desertion of those they most trusted.

Abuse makes everything appear unsafe. One of abuse's most deleterious aspects is that it sabotages the very trust that makes us susceptible to love and healing. This sorrow, if unattended, may persist throughout life.

Though there is no quick fix for the loss of trust, after some time of sending a merciful awareness into the pain, it will begin to displace at least some of our distrust with something much more beautiful and more liberating.

The processing of our grief can take many forms. Although one might benefit from meditations such as forgiveness and techniques such as heart speech or tapping at the grief point to convert it to the touch point of the heart (which we'll cover in detail in the coming pages), there is also an intuition for healing, a kind whisper from the still small voice within, that can guide us toward wholeness.

In the case of forgiving, and thus finishing business with the departed, we are only limited by our distrust in our intuition and lack of imagination. I have seen many imaginative rituals devised to restore trust. An extreme but very practical example was of a woman, who, still badly bruised from abuse as a child after years of therapy, made thirty large photographic copies of her father's face after he died and covered a whole wall in her home as "an altar to my healing." Each day for several weeks she had a ritual defacing until the screaming and ripping and the blacking-out of eyes and mouth subsided. Finally, she began to draw with crayon, as a very young child might, stick figures of a house and family, the father of which was gradually invited over the days somewhat closer to the rest of the family. She said that after a while, instead of attacking him, she began singing aloud to herself. And the song became about her accepting her rage at him as being perfectly reasonable and not at all any discredit to the possibilities of "my brand-new heart" slowly revealing itself to her in the depths of such once-resisted self-acceptance. She later said that, oddly enough,

"The healing month had been a turnaround. I had to forgive myself first for not trusting what I felt, and somehow recognize that this shame I was carrying rightly belonged to someone else.

"And I cried at his grave. I don't even know why. Maybe I was crying for what I never had. So I began forgiving his wretched, alcohol-poisoned brain that could not contain its pain and spewed it out onto everyone around. And it reminded me to be kinder, to leave less ruin in my wake."

Trust is one of the first things to go and one of the last to return.

Trust returns as slowly as a frightened child to a dark room. It returns in increments as we find ourselves capable of relating to our wounds a bit more mindfully and a lot more heartfully. By noting how fear gives rise to the demons that at times assail us, breaking down fear into its elements, and observing it from moment to moment with a kindness that wants us only to be free, we see how fear, even distrust, is workable. We must trust our distrust enough to approach it with a mercy that was absent from its origins.

Still, as trust returns, it has to overcome fantasies that life is somehow supposed to be in our control and that we are at fault when it is not. We must come to trust the process of healing enough to open our heart to the unknown. We must acknowledge its unpredictable unfolding with a sense of compassion for ourselves and others who tremble at the brink of what comes next, whether it's tragedy or grace. And we must remember that somehow our heart has room for it all.

Mercy breaks all the rules.

Some of the most skillful therapists and caregivers I know learned the lessons of love from a loveless childhood, both the terrible lessons that tore into the heart and the wonderful lessons that eventually healed it.

Trust returns from success in self-inquiry, perhaps from spiritual empowerment. It also returns after being loved long enough to feel loved.

It would of course be foolish to put "blind faith" in the future, but we can put faith in the work we do on ourselves. Confidence is cultivated from the sudden wordless understandings of insights we believed ourselves unworthy to receive and from the hard work, perhaps the hardest work we shall ever do, to let go of our suffering. Confidence grows from the unexpected, at first even distrusted, effects of a gradual forgiveness that lightens our burden; from experiments in mercy and a gradual increase in mindfulness. We discover that we are capable of relating to our pain instead of only suffering from it. And that growth in confidence acts as a counterbalance to our loss of trust in the world as we discover a greater trust in ourselves.

The mind has within it savagery and grace, cold indifference to the pain of others, and a warmth that flows toward those in difficulty. Viewing the physical and psychological damage that is the outcome of violence, our concern for the well-being of others flows like a river into fire.

As the Dalai Lama said when asked of what earthly use could all the pain in the world be, "Without pain there would be no compassion."

In a series of dreams I had, I saw myself as the victim of great abuse and then experienced myself as the horrific abuser. In the first I felt great pity for myself; in the latter, great disgust. As I explored each in myself,

MAY ALL BEINGS BE AT PEACE.

an empathy arose for both: a balance that soothed the causes of righ-teous revenge in one and almost suicidal guilt in the other. And after the emotional shock of being both the abuser and the abused was tended to, a quiet settled over the battlefield and peace was proposed.

Gradually, with mercy and awareness, we can reinhabit our life—not the old life, but a new one.

7

THE MEANING
OF LIFE

THE MEANING OF LIFE CHANGES WHEN WE CONFRONT
LOSS. Our search for meaning and purpose leaves us wandering and
bewildered. What was ordinary yesterday becomes precious today, and
what was precious yesterday seems dull and lusterless. What we liked
becomes uninteresting, but what we loved becomes everything.

There is a delicate balance that we need to honor as we try to "find
meaning" in any event or state of mind: Many people confuse *finding
meaning* with finding *a reason*, putting our finger on something or
someone for blame.

Meaning contains many different qualities and characteristics; it means the significance of events as much as their causes. Meaning is an attempt to decipher the bittersweet world, at making sense, giving order, to the seemingly random twist of things. It is a plea for the completion of incomplete loose ends.

Without meaning, life has no direction, so we scramble through the stars to augur an acceptable future. Actually, the mind seeks a *reason* (a cause, a blame), so the *meaning* (which can make sense of it) can be found in the heart. We are looking for a cosmic coincidence to interpret it all, to reinforce that there is any meaning to everything after all.

For many people, finding meaning may be the redefinition of a loss in a way that's necessary for "closure." Many believe closure is a finalization of grief, but actually it is a changing of levels at which loss is experienced, an opening into the letting go that is letting be, an integration of the pain into the heart. It is making peace with loss. Closure, a level of finishing unfinished business, is the term often used by survivors of a violent crime when the antagonist is punished. But for most people, the wound is not so obvious, and more than *meaning* may be required.

A psychotherapist friend of mine spoke of his work with people in grief and crisis and his attempts to help them "decipher their lives." He tried to help them find some meaning in their situations that they could be satisfied with, which he found did help them in accepting the loss at one stage. But, noticing that an appreciable part of what they were reaching for was some supernatural meaning, he came to feel that supporting them too long at this level of meaning might be keeping them from going deeper, from directly addressing their pain.

He felt that bargaining with their pain and settling for some significance, though momentarily comforting, might actually be delaying their healing and might ultimately reinforce their suffering by keeping them stuck at the same level from which feelings of "the meaninglessness of life" also arise. He said "meaning" is okay as far as it goes, but it doesn't go far enough to liberate people from their suffering. He felt a merciful awareness that goes "deeper than meaning," that trusts the "don't know" openness and simplicity of mind before the rush to knowing—that is, to meaning—was necessary for us to join the hunt for our true selves, for what he called "true healing." The clutter of our knowing, of our preconceptions and our assumptions, keeps the mind from knowing itself at a deeper and more reliable level. It keeps the mind from a truth, my friend said, that tears us open and somehow puts us back together again stronger and more loving than before, more able to confront, yet still embrace, all that passes for "reality."

When we experience loss, we question the meaning of our birth and death and insist that the answer has to come from some suprarational source. But it is difficult to uncover it from this perspective. The meaning of life has to come from within us. And the most satisfying of those meanings always arise from love: the love of others, the love of work, the love of God, the love of the pilgrimage toward the heart, the love of the art and science of self-discovery. It is from love's absence that the world often seems the most meaningless.

In a life that many people say would not be worth living if it had no meaning, we discover that the meaning of life is the meaning we offer to it—the aspiration to know the whole of our being. We can uncover no secret from on high that will reveal to us at last the reason we so often seem to be discomforted.

As life continues to change, the question "Who am I, and what am I doing here?" peels back layers and layers of what we took for granted to see what was bestowed upon us at birth: the potential for going beyond our ordinary and extraordinary suffering to reveal something worth living for, the peace and compassion that compose the nucleus of being.

Martin felt his life had lost its center and that nothing made sense anymore. He said,

"I remember in high school math, they spoke of the theoretical limit. I think I reached the theoretical limit of my pain with the death of my son. It was all the pain I could bear and still stay alive. A life once so full was drained of meaning.

"I found myself spending a lot of time in prayer and contemplation. It was the only context big enough for this longing for my son and all the confusion it brought up. Not knowing what anything meant or even what to do next, but not quite wanting to kill my-self, I just let myself die into this unknowing."

How we approach our not knowing what comes next is what gives meaning to our lives.

When we wholeheartedly surrender into our not knowing, into what students of meditation refer to as "don't know mind" (the apotheosis of open mindedness) by not clinging to or condemning anything in the passing show of consciousness, but simply letting it flow unhindered, an openness and vulnerability to deeper and deeper truth rises from our inborn unknown wisdom. The truth that is exposed seems somehow already so deeply known, yet the surprise of its diamond clarity over-whelms one with humility and gratitude.

In that stillness—in that space between breaths, between thoughts, between lives—something is suddenly remembered, something it seems impossible to ever have forgotten. And in every fiber of our being we know that love is the only rational act of a lifetime.

Then, what may have seemed like "meaningless loss," though it does not hurt any less, often leads to meaningful *change*, which, like every evolutionary leap, must cross seemingly uncrossable chasms.

8

IN THE ABSENCE
OF GOD

OUR SEARCH FOR MEANING COMES FROM THE LOSS OF
MEANING, perhaps a loss of God. The loss of a loved one, for many
people, feels like an abandonment by God. Anger at God can unfortunately become an immediate as well as a long-range begrudging, an
acute as well as chronic loss of faith.

Some say love is as close as we get to God without really trying.
When we experience love and have an open heart, the world becomes
almost preternaturally alive. But when the heart is obscured by the
death or betrayal of a loved one, the world seems cold and lifeless.

There is no one we hate more than someone we once loved who we feel betrayed us. Indeed, in some divorces never is there expressed such vitriolic recriminations as by those who were once very much in love. We can have those same feelings toward God. When we feel God has reneged on what we imagined was our pious bargain, we throw God out of our heart. We curse God's inattentiveness and indifferent response to our pleadings.

The broken devotee crying out to their God says, "My life has been full of hardship. Only intermittent moments of love kept me alive. I cannot speak Your name without feeling cast away."

A love, stronger than our fear of death, which gave so much meaning to our lives at its zenith, can turn sour with that same intensity at its nadir. And what was once so meaningful seems an apparition.

We say God is dead when the personal self, the thought "I am This," with all its anger and self-obsession, blocks the universal Self, the sense "I am That." But when that individual remembers itself as part of a much larger whole, God, or whatever passes for it, comes into view.

God is not dead—we are. I had a teacher some years ago who used to say, "You are already dead! And so is everyone you love! How long will you wait to tell them, to embrace them, to listen more? What do you fear more than losing this heart shared with all that is?"

The mercy we may not feel from God might come instead from ourselves when we recognize how much random discomfort attends our daily activities, how a barely definable suffering underlies each half-taken breath. When the heart reminds us just how much softening into kindness expands the context in which we unfold, it becomes our true self for which we search. And we undertake a pilgrimage, which can last for days or months or years and may take us halfway around the world or to the center of the universe. The sojourn is from forgetfulness to awakening, from the stolid mind to the clarity of the open heart through which we pass on our way into the peace that surpasses understanding.

Our pilgrimages may take us down the path with a heart to Benares or Lourdes, to the Haj or Jerusalem, or to a local church or a favorite tree in a beloved woods. It may take us for perhaps a few miles' walk, blending step after step with the breath, to a nearby house of worship or natural power spot. It may bid us enter with the innocence of one who has never been there before, as one for whom the world has changed and perhaps, quite against their will, become new, as one who is ready to look for a moment with their true heart into our great and perniciously imperceptible suffering. And sitting quietly we notice how very alive we are, that death passes, but love and gratitude remain.

On one such foray onto the fields of a merciful awareness, it was a great day in my life when I knew for myself that God was love, and neither the unnamable Presence we call God nor the indecipherable sentience we call self is dead. And there's a sense that it never will be.

Sometimes the pilgrimage through our suffering feels as though we are being "skinned alive," as Craig put it after losing his young daughter to a rare heart attack the year before. He said ever since his loss he felt as though he had to live "in the agonizing absence of God."

"At one point, at the worst of it, I went up to the top of a mountain and just screamed at the universe. And something snapped. Coming down from there I had the most beautiful walk. There was radiant sunshine; leaves were luminous, translucent. God was everywhere.

"And on the way down I met an angel in the form of a woman, and as she passed me on the trail she touched my hand and said, 'Hold your heart softly.'

"I didn't know who she was, but at that moment I knew what I had to do. For so long I was so sad and angry, waiting to find myself.

"At that moment there arose an insight that has often sustained me since the days got long and I was more lost than found. It doesn't sound like much when I put it into words, but when it causes my heart to tremble it means everything. It was, 'God is never absent, only we are.' I may sit and count my breaths to concentrate my mind, or go for a walk to mindfully reinhabit my body, or sit in a quiet corner rocking in rhythm with a certain song that is sacred to me going in my mind, until the breath disappears into the song and the song sings itself as if from the lips of a loved one. And there It is, there is God as love for the stranger across the aisle, for the occupants of the building burning on the evening news, for that poor soul's reflection sliding across the store windows as I pass."

Sometimes we can find God quite easily. Sometimes not at all. Sometimes our heart is like the sun. Sometimes the heart is like a stone. Such loss is among our deepest griefs. Some say we can never find God, but only be still until God finds us. Only "be still and know."

9

WHEN THE MIRROR OF THE HEART IS BROKEN

WHEN WE LOVE SOMEONE, THEY BECOME A MIRROR FOR OUR HEART. They reflect back to us the place within us that is love, the divine principle. When that mirror is shattered through death or separation, we may feel as though love itself has died.

We may not even know where our next breath will come from. We are afflicted by wave after wave of sadness and distress. All we can do is sit quietly and count our breaths, inhaling mercy, exhaling fear. Slowly, we cultivate self-mercy in order to overcome the violence that contaminates our dreams, breathing in whatever mercy and forgiveness is available, breathing out the sorrow.

Sometimes the out-breath seems so long. It's so hard to let go!

When we lose a loved one, there is, at first, a great tearing away, a breaking away of every certainty. Through fluorescent hospital corridors, sunlit cemeteries, and endless condolences, none of the explanations or prayers seem to suffice. There remains the feeling that our loved one might walk through the door at any moment. It all seems so unjust, as over the months and years they are not standing where they should be, don't speak up where they used to, don't laugh when we do.

One morning, as I washed my cereal bowl, I noticed a crack across one side. It reminded me of one Buddhist master's teaching that "the glass is already broken." And the mirror, too, I thought. He said that though a crystal goblet given to him earlier in the day seemed so everlastingly beautiful, so able to catch the sun, impermanence was always encroaching; it was just a matter of time before gravity pulled it from the table or the winds of change blew it off the shelf and it would lie at his feet as a scattering of shards. In the same way that "this glass is already broken," all that we love will someday turn to dust. But the love will remain. A love that calls us even now to attend more fully as much to the sorrow remaining from a departed loved one as to the unloved parts of ourselves.

A woman who said all she could feel within her was the loss of her dead husband remarked,

"All the holy books I've read seem to say that the kingdom of heaven is within, that finding my Buddha Nature will make me eternally happy, but all that big stuff seems to elude me right now. I haven't been able to catch sight of that in a very long time.

"But working for the past months to soften my belly, to loosen the tightness on my heart, once in a while everything sort of melts into the background and nothing is in pain. There is a glimpse of big silence.

"But there does seem to be something beneath the sorrow, something not really big and strong but something in me that really wants to feel better and even help others feel better.

"And I feel a little better. But to tell the truth, I would rather be with Robert than with God."

A GRIEF JOURNAL

If we were to go to a business that sells mirrors and ask them to repair a broken mirror, they would say it's not worth the trouble because they would have to fill and polish the area—and still a slight ripple would follow the crack and cause something of a distortion in the reflection. They would advise us to get a new mirror. But in grief it is the mind that is the mirror and not so easily disposed of.

By looking into the fracturing of the mirror of the mind and regularly noting the fissures on its surface, perhaps in a grief journal, we can begin to polish with mercy whatever incompletely repaired reflection distorts our worldview. Writing out our hearts is an ongoing refinement of subtler aspects of our sense of connection and disconnection. We can begin to repair our mirror.

Sometimes, we write as a means of opening the conduit between the mind and the heart. Writing what we feel while we are feeling it is a means of inviting what is sometimes the ghost of ourselves out of the shadows. When we write, we become open to unexpected insight and spontaneous guidance from our "still small voice within." It becomes a daily exercise in self-exploration and expression. The willingness to explore our suffering, to find what habitual paths it takes, moves the pen, finds the words, and doodles the soul in the margins. We continually find that the journal writes itself when given half a chance. As we drive to work or walk to meet friends, thoughts arise—inspirations, almost— of what might be written in the journal on its next opening. And this reflection on what we feel and how it might be expressed deepens insight into our process—that is, the unfolding of our "way of being" and the natural forward motion of our evolution.

Anna, freshly returned to a less constricted life, said,

"I went to the place where my son drowned, and I stood with a friend. And later she said, 'Come on. I'll buy you a journal and you can write.' And I said no. I started crying. I said I couldn't write. I've never been able to write in a journal before. And then, at some point last winter, when he had been dead six months or so, I began to write. And it became kind of like automatic writing. It just came out."

Maybe it's time for you to keep a grief journal. In the expression of your sorrow and doubt, the words carry us beyond the time when the mind addresses the heart and fear appeals for mercy. Writing in a grief journal combines the past and the future in this single moment. What I mean is that if we open our journals ten years from now, that same healing will await us. What will come into view as we reread our moments is a sense of process—that all these feelings have arisen before and are on each occasion welcomed with some less difficulty, as each cycle holds less sway over us.

When we reread the passages, we are less lost in their content, in *what* they say. We instead see these afflictive thoughts more as part of a process: anger as blocked desire, fear as loss of control, doubt as agitated distrust. They occur all by themselves. States of mind arise quite uninvited. They follow the leader, the strongest feeling out of the gate.

Ondrea and I know a number of people who keep track of even more specific states than just the broad band of suffering we call grief. They keep anger journals. They are so willing to heal that they'll try anything.

Whether it's foolish, or even irrational, whatever the flow, they just keep writing.

Another insight that is exposed when we reread our journals is the hallucinatory quality of sadness: we discover that its insistence that we've never been this sad before is a hollow deception. When we look at page ninety-three, at page forty-one, at page six, we notice a certain quality to these states of mind that tends to mislead us. We have been this way before.

Such afflictive states of mind are constantly giving us false information about what to do with them: "Push me away! Run for your life!" But if we take their advice, these states will only get stronger. Look how strong they have already become by just following that strategy!

There's a natural urgency that keeps us stuck, making us think that it's never going to go away: "I've got to get rid of it." In a way, grief lasts a lifetime, but it is up to us whether we close around that pain and it diminishes our life or we open it to include not just our pain but the pain we share with all sentient beings—a life lived huddled in the corner or a life exposed to love and healing.

A grief journal is a tool to find our way through the darkness now. It is also a compass to direct us past pitfalls later on when we reread it. We'll know the terrain a bit better and be a bit less liable to get lost.

I should note that it is not just our very personal mind that causes all this suffering but something in the given nature of the mind itself. We see that in the mindful observation of our reflection in the mirror. We possess a quite involuntary negative attachment to pain, which, when we try to push it away, mires us deeper. Unfortunately, this is a natural part of our case of mistaken identity we call ego—the part of us in the mirror that, unless more fully explored, finds in these relatively superficial, though excessively painful, layers of thought and emotion little more than itself. This part of our brain has long employed pain to make itself feel real. It's quite a predicament, but bringing a liberating awareness, an increasingly freeing perception, into such painful tendencies is what the Buddha called "the work to be done."

10

A BAD DREAM

MANY PEOPLE SPEAK OF THE FIRST STAGES OF ACUTE GRIEF—
particularly when it's from an unexpected loss due to sudden medical failure,
accident, or violence—like it is a bad dream. There is a feeling of unreality
about it. Shock implodes the mental construct of our lives. We find it difficult to tell what is real, yet it takes a while to adjust to a different reality.

A well-known example of this unreality is the story of the collapse of
a concrete walkway in a Kansas City hotel, under which a mother and
her six-year-old son were pinned for some hours. Every few minutes, he
asked her if it was a dream.

Mark had a similar reaction during the reeling period after the death
of his wife.

"Lately my life has been like a dream I had where I was talking with my wife who had recently died. I was enjoying our conversation so much when I realized, much to my dismay, 'This is a dream.'

"Waking, I turned to her and started telling her about the dream, until I realized I was still dreaming. And once again I came to the surface, but this time I got out of bed to make sure I would not fall back asleep. Then I laughed with her, telling her how I had thought I was awake but had still been dreaming—and then I recognized I was still dreaming.

"Each time I came to the surface, instead of waking and actually getting out of bed, I fell back into the dream and just dreamed I was awaking to her lost presence. It got so I didn't know if I was awake or not. It wasn't difficult to say, 'This is a dream,' but even when I tested my awakening, by sitting up and crossing my legs and saying, 'This certainly is not a dream,' I was still dreaming.

"When I actually woke up a bit later, a slightly dazed morning followed. Sometimes I said to myself, 'This is not a dream,' but I was never quite sure if that was true . . . and never quite sure she was gone."

Some spiritual teachers say that when our expectations are challenged, we are shaken from what we have been dreaming. We may awake with a start, unable to quite tell the past from the present.

There is an old belief that to awaken someone too suddenly when they are sleepwalking might cause them such a shock as to cause them harm. In no circumstance may this be truer than in being forced out of our dream that things are other than they really are. It is a dream that calls for a gradual awakening.

Though this difficulty waking is often called denial, because of the difficulty accepting a painful truth, there is beneath the surface a very dynamic state unfolding.

Occasionally we hear someone speak about a friend they believe must be "rescued from denial," who won't acknowledge their pain. We wonder why anyone would wish to take another's denial away and destroy the buffer zone beneath the surface in which so much may be working itself out in its own time. To take away a person's denial is to take away their dignity. Denial is a survival mechanism when very few others remain. It's not wholly unskillful. It disperses as recognition and acceptance deepens. Indeed, in this sense, "denial" is recognized as a not uncommon early reaction to painful events, understood to be a not unhealthy first response to pain in the natural unfolding of grief. It may only become a problem when we are unable to get by it or use it as a continuing anesthetizing agent.

There is perhaps no clearer manifestation of grief than numbness. When the pain is too great, just too much for the available wiring, we shut down rather than short-circuit. We implode rather than explode.

Where we expect to find a highly sensitive area around pain, we may discover it is actually going numb from overload. This is as true of a broken bone as it is a broken heart. At the periphery of the pain, whether it is grief or a migraine, we pass into unconsciousness. The no-man's-land of unresolved issues, the difficulty incorporating a loss as great as our love, disguises itself as barren ground. Some speak of losses so great the shock has numbed them. They've closed off.

This numbness at the edge is the unattended sorrow. It's all the places where we've gone numb and allowed that numbness to deepen, over-flowing the walls by which we attempt to compartmentalize our pain. Our grief is submerged like submarine whose heavy, watertight doors close off and isolate a flooded compartment. Unattended sorrow is the hardness at the edge not being met by anything soft.

At one time or another in our personal evolution, denial may have been all we had. It is an awkward blessing that shelters some, particu-larly children, from the storm. But, at another time in our evolution, it becomes an obstacle.

So, we watch for the places that are numb. We start to accept denial. We forgive it and thank it, realizing with a shiver that if all of a sudden all of our denial were removed, we would be frozen in place in abject terror. If we didn't have some degree of denial, some buffer zone against reality, we'd never get in a car or on an airplane. We'd never step off the curb. We wouldn't have children. We'd never go bungee jumping or get into a relationship because they are just too dangerous and too uncertain. Our denial keeps the planet going.

Much work is done in dreams. We can once again speak with, hold, or lose our loved ones who are long since departed. We can retrieve the love unexpressed or unreceived. It's another opportunity for us to wake from drowsy reassertions of fear, another opportunity to finish business. So much of our unfinished business is a result of acting compulsively, mechanically, from a half-conscious dream state, that sometimes it takes a dream to bring it to our attention.

11

OPENING THE HEART IN HELL

GRIEF CALLS US TO OPEN OUR HEART IN HELL.

When hope is wounded and life spins out of our control—when we're stunned from bewilderment and dismay—our nerve endings seemingly burst into flame, and the chemicals in our brain become a witch's brew.

When our old escape routes from pain have been cut off, when our grief is undeniable, we move like a blind person through a maze, feeling our way forward, slowly, mercifully, soft-bellied through our grief. Approaching with mercy and loving kindness that which we have always withdrawn from in fear, judgment, doubt, and distrust, there arises the possibility for the healing of a lifetime.

Statements like "Grief can have a quality of healing about it" may seem absurd in the midst of a dark night of the soul. Such phrases seem like merely good-intentioned drivel in the face of a crushing loss. They appear to be nothing more than clichés meant to suppress the natural unfolding of unpredictably raw emotions. But in truth, because we are forced to a depth of feeling that is usually well below the threshold of our awareness, where many of our least productive attitudes and motivations arise, there are life healings available in insights into how we have abandoned our pain most of our lives—insights into how clever we have become at disguising our unattended sorrow, no longer surprised by how long, and in how many ways, our unresolved grief has acted itself out in anger and depression, in oversensitivity and numbness.

The inclination to disown our pain degrades us and turns our pain into suffering. Approaching the pain with mercy and awareness, we are called to open our hearts to it.

Hell is resistance. Much of this resistance to the moment, to life itself, this long-reinforced unwillingness to experience the unpleasant, can be noticed as a hardness in the belly. When we are angry or frightened or confused, our belly turns to concrete; when we are loving, unrecognized fear floats in unexpected mercy and our belly becomes like an ocean.

When we can accept even the unacceptable, when we can open even to our pain, that surrender frees us from hell. We may feel awful, but opening around the sensations of tightness in our body releases our holding. And in that release we are more readily able to relate *to* these feelings instead of only *from* them, to begin to investigate them instead of only reacting blindly to them. It is the exploration of our under-worlds that teaches us to let go of hell. And in that letting go we dis-cover that heaven is simply the absence of hell.

I don't know anyone whose heart is open all the time, whose heart is never even vaguely mottled by the grief of loneliness or doubt. We are learning to open our hearts, even to our hearts being sometimes closed, to forgive ourselves for not being more forgiving, to care for ourselves even though we may at times be uncaring, to have mercy on how mer-ciless we can be. It is from this perspective that we learn to be loving by watching how unloving we can be.

Indeed, the phrase "opening the heart" can be a bit misleading, for "the heart" is actually a level of mind. The heart does not so much open as become available. It is a natural state we experience when it is no longer obscured by unattended sorrow. A true heart is an inherent con-dition of our underlying nature.

The word "heart," as often as any other intended meaning, also in-corporates the source of unconditional love. Although many people commonly designate the heart as the traditional source of emotion, these upwellings are more a product of a somewhat narrower, though intensely affecting, level of mind.

Many people have said that if they are being totally honest, their hearts are not open but two or three minutes in a day or even two or three minutes in a week. But what we don't realize is that in this forgetful world it is a miracle the heart is open at all. It's a wonder that the level of awareness we call the heart is not totally submerged by waves of fear, judgment, aggrandizement, and negation.

As a teacher of mine once said, "The mind creates the abyss and the heart crosses it." Love is the bridge.

We take the next step across the span that bridges the broken heart because there is little else that honors our relationship with a lost loved one or ourselves. It takes courage to trust the process of surrendering our sorrow. It is so painful to open that fist of resistance cramped about the heart. We peel back the pain, one finger at a time, but slowly our openness returns. It is the pain that ends pain. It is the mercy that expands into loving kindness.

To open our hearts in hell we must be willing to relinquish our long-conditioned, ever-merciless insistence on judging all that passes through the senses. Liking this and disliking that, habitual preference flitting back and forth from one object of seeing, hearing, tasting, smelling, feeling, or thinking, to another. We have turned our back on ourselves in judgment so often, we have come to see ourselves as "other" at times and exemplify the statement, "Judge not lest you be judged!" The judging mind sees everyone as other; it doesn't really differentiate between you and the person next to you.

When grief doubles back on us and amplifies loss by judging our moments of confusion unkindly, we see how uncompassionate we can be with ourselves. And once again, it is seeing into the nature of our hell that directs us toward heaven. We need to forgive ourselves for occasionally being more desirous of love than able to offer it, and for our simple foolishness when we thought we were right or were sure they were wrong. We need to forgive ourselves and God for breaking the bargain made all too long just below the breath. We need to stop rehearsing for Judgment Day.

No judgment that we might fear from on high is more caustic than our capacity to mercilessly ridicule ourselves.

It is not love that judges us but the models of perfection to which we cling. Concepts of perfection assail us with feelings of imperfection. This is a teaching that it seems we must sometimes go through hell to discover.

Though we may be disappointed by how many times we missed the mark and lost an opportunity to heal ourselves and others, the teaching is clear: Love is the highest form of acceptance, and judgment is the hard rejection of that acceptance.

When mercy embraces the wounded sense of self, the heart traverses the time it takes in timelessness for us to accept and forgive ourselves.

12

THE TRAUMA
OF SURVIVAL

WHEN WE SURVIVE THE CATASTROPHE OF ANOTHER'S DEATH, whether the cause is accident, illness, or violence, it is not unusual to feel survivor's sorrow in the form of guilt.

"Two months ago I watched my best friend die," said Adrian, saying he felt as though he had let go of his end of the lifeline.

"I find myself more and more alone, as opposed to more and more open to the people around me. The person I lost was the one whom I confided in most, and I'm afraid to even ask someone else for help because I'm afraid that I'm going to lose them too. I don't think it's about abandonment. I do have issues surrounding abandonment, as most people probably do, but I feel that's not the problem. It's not about abandonment; it's about not being able to go with them."

When we survive the death of a loved one, we need to carefully watch the tendency to become cruel to ourselves, as in, "Why did I survive and she didn't?" When we berate ourselves, our minds recall our unskillful actions, our forgetfulness and selfishness, our pettiness and emotional dishonesty in the past, just to demonstrate the unequal justice of God's will.

Guilt, at times, causes us to call out, "God, are you sure it was him instead of me you wanted to take?" Survivor's remorse causes us to say, "I should have done more." But we can't! We can't stop anyone we love from dying! Our children, our parents, our lovers, and our friends will all die someday.

The unattended sorrow of the survivor is now often referred to as delayed, or post-traumatic, stress syndrome. But it may not encompass only our feelings that we survived while others did not. It may be a kind of dismay that we survive at all.

A friend of mine in high school was shot in a movie theater by someone fidgeting with a gun in the seat behind him. It changed his life. Though he almost died, he eventually made what the doctors—but not he—considered a complete recovery. For a year or so afterward, particularly in times of stress, he tended to look over his shoulder. Long after the bullet was removed, his mental wound continued to fester. His grief was over the loss of innocence, safety, and trust in an unreliable future looming just around the next unknown corner.

From such a trauma, deeper psychological wounds may persist. Long after the shrapnel is removed, the inner war continues. Long after that dreadful phone call from the highway patrol, the jumpiness and the hypervigilance over our shoulder remain. We may no longer feel safe anywhere. What was once a bedrock of meaning in our lives may become a mire of regret and confusion; we may even feel we're being punished by the gods for not being somehow "good" enough. Not unusual things like a car's backfire, a phone ringing in the next room, or a jet plane passing overhead may at least momentarily inflame the senses.

Time freezes, as one man who had fought in Vietnam and later became a policeman observes: "Sometimes, in the thick of things, you may not even know you were hit until afterward, and sometimes it can take months, even years, before we find out how deep that wound might be."

These sentiments are not unique to any one war. Most of our fathers who fought in a war came home in the condition once called "shell-shocked." Many, to some degree, manifested some sort of delayed stress syndrome. My father never saw combat, but he was trained in the First World War in how to kill large numbers with chemical warfare. Ondrea's father barely survived the Battle of the Bulge and still speaks of it fifty-seven years later as if it were yesterday. Still, he sees his best friend frozen at his machine gun. Still, he feels the sting of bullets tearing away his jacket. The twentieth century, like most centuries pre-

ceding, was created and informed by the many people who barely survived wars and famines and left the stamp of their unresolved grief on
the legacy that their daughters and sons were to live through, the shock-
wave passing through generation after generation.

CRAWLING OUT
FROM UNDER DEATH

When we survive an event that others did not, sometimes the reason we
don't know quite where to put our feet is that we can't even believe we
still have feet.

That kind of confusion can so distract the mind that we lose the path
toward the heart. Nothing makes any sense. We discover that "peace of
mind" is a contradiction in terms. We are either at peace or we are lost
in the twisting corridors of the mind.

The trauma of survival after the loss of a loved one, as well as the daily
fear of survival, swims just below the surface. We share a communal
grief about those who never made it through the day as we crawl out
from under multiple deaths in the evening news, the repeated images of
the falling Twin Towers on 9/11, and the brutality of the wars constantly
being fought on the scarred surface of this rapidly diminishing planet.
We do not have to outlive a loved one or survive a catastrophe to feel

some level of neglected responsibility for the "victims of happenstance" on the six o'clock "Survivor's News." Whether it's families consumed by fire, the woeful conditions of an old age home, or the desperation in the eyes of a mother trying to sustain her children in a battered-women's shelter, our empathy and helplessness are drawn down deep.

When we hear about the Holocaust or the Oklahoma City bombing, or when we see the faces of the left-behind loved ones after the Twin Towers collapsed, our heart resonates with all the other hearts broken by cruel coincidence. Ironically, survivor's guilt is filled with compassion for the plight of others, sometimes unfortunately so much so that it fills the mind with hopelessness and fear and tears down all our safeguards, leaving us feeling extremely vulnerable and directionless.

The same sad, self-punishing truth exhibits itself in any catastrophe, whether it is the multiple deaths of friends in a single event such as an automobile accident or the slow attrition of one's community through epidemics such as the carnage of AIDS. James, bent under years of loss, said:

"In 1982 I lost my first friend to AIDS. By 1986, I had lost over fifty, and I stopped counting.

"I went and got a nursing degree, and now my job is helping people to die—to hold them, to help them let go. I don't have any belief in reincarnation, and I have some difficulty understanding some of those things, but I certainly believe that there's a definite spiritual process happening when they die. I've seen it leave the body. I don't know where it goes, but it leaves.

"It must be in the hundreds that I've lost. Daily, weekly, I watch in them my parents, my children, my friends, my lovers die. They're my brothers and my sisters!"

When others have died and we are still around to tell the tale, we may believe we have survived "for a purpose." And once again, we are right for the wrong reason, because it is not a new "purpose" but rather an opportunity to investigate the perhaps inborn purpose, whose source is worth a lifetime's exploration, that has offered to guide us our whole lives.

There is little that raises the level of the reservoir of grief as sudden death does. And there's no news more shocking than the death of one who killed herself. What is particularly rueful is the suicide of a person so overwhelmed by sorrow that she felt her only remedy was to not feel, that only death would suffice. Few losses are more difficult to integrate or more demanding to wholly resolve, leaving in their wake so much guilt and powerlessness. Few deaths leave more internal dialogue, more alternative possibilities. "I should have seen it coming. I should have called that night. I should have loved more or prayed harder or danced with her more." Always another "should," always another culpable misperception left uncorrected.

Many people pass their sorrow along, hanging their skeleton in another's closet.

This certainly was the case with Tesha, whose mother committed suicide, an act from which Tesha never fully recovered.

"I was six years old when my mother died, and my father chose not to tell us the truth. He said she had died of a reaction to penicillin. Every time I would ask the family about her, they would cry, so I stopped asking. I didn't learn the truth until I was in my thirties. I'm going to be forty-two this year, and there is a first grader still inside me who can hardly read but is expected to keep the end of the world to herself.

"And because of the conspiracy of silence in my family, I lived a lie for most of my youth. I lost track of my life."

When our faith in life is tested, facing our pain with mercy and awareness gives purpose to our lives.

Everyone still alive is a survivor. And the price of survival is the grief and praise and lamentation and delight for what has come before, for what has led us to this very moment. And here we are alive and sad, alive and happy, alive and confused—bewildered, but alive. Not that those who have died are not alive too and perhaps also feeling something of survivor's guilt for leaving the rest of us behind.

13

CONNECTION

IN OUR GRIEF, WE CANNOT IMAGINE that there's any such thing as feeling other than we do.

At first, all we experience is the separation: "I'm not going to see them, touch them, smell them again." Sometimes we think maybe we'd kill ourselves if it weren't for our children playing in the next room.

Even there, in that absence, something happens as we let that pain into our mind and body, as we soften to it. What we now call grief—that sense of absolute absence, of incredible sadness, of difficulty taking the next breath—can settle into a place of enduring connectedness with the departed.

Though it may now seem impossible at times, grief does have a beginning, middle, and something like an end, which is actually more of a new beginning, another level of relating to that departed loved one. It isn't that the relationship ends; it's just the hardest edge of the suffering that subsides. In the beginning of the grief process, we might feel that person is "a million miles away." They seem irretrievable, but eventually they reenter our heart at another level, and most often we feel a sense of warmth and closeness.

We become inseparable from that person. At first, fear and sorrow drown the mind. Thoughts of all that has departed, memories of what was, and fantasies of what might have been weigh down our thoughts. But eventually that separation seems to melt into the essential connection that joined us in the first place. There is a sense of unbreakable unity.

Love is never lost.

Grief changes in intensity and duration as it becomes integrated into the heart. As one woman said when asked where her dead child was, "He is in my eyes and in my bones." Our departed loved ones live in our marrow. Twenty-five years from now, when you smell that same smell of antiseptic gauze, it will take you right back to your dear one's hospital bed, or when you smell that same smell of vanilla, it will take you right back to your mother's kitchen before she passed on. Smells will often do that. It may only be for a few minutes, but that grief is momentarily as fresh as when we heard the last breath leave our loved one's body. Attending to our unattended sorrow opens the way to a new life.

A most skillful means of finding closure, of finishing business, is encouraged when we call to our departed loved one using the essentially intuitive process called "heart speech," and send blessings directly from our heart to theirs. (This is also sometimes used when working with a person who's in a coma.) Meeting deeply in the heart so that we might say good-bye without ever loosing our connection, wishing them well on their journey, and integrating our grief into a love and concern for that other's well-being aids in clearing the path ahead for ourselves. And who knows what value it might actually hold for the departed to help them finish their business as well.

There are elements of heart speech that resemble the "business finishing" content and intention of a grief journal. Using the practice of connecting with another silently, intuitively, feeling as one might when singing a child to sleep, we speak into another's heart as an expansion of our own continued healing. Heart speech is often employed in the time-honored practice of talking to the dead.

Our relationship with the departed is not over; it has just changed dimensions. Keep talking to them, and don't be too surprised if you seem to hear them answer. Grief is not a time to be too rational. This silent heart speech may last a lifetime. It soothes us.

We sense that when people die, they continue on, so we speak to them in our hearts, feeling beyond time and loss a certain timelessness that even death cannot diminish. From our heartfelt knowing that only love can cross the abyss, we tell them we'll be along soon. We'll all be along soon. We are spirit clothed in body. Though the body wears through, can become threadbare, and is easily torn, the spirit is deathless and indestructible. The ever-transferable life force is as formless as light.

As I write of the power of heart speech, one experience in particular comes to mind that reinforced my confidence in the potential of this practice. When serving as a pastoral care counselor in a hospital, I was asked to work with a dying patient who was in and out of lucidity due to cirrhosis of the liver. It turned out he did not speak English, and my Spanish is negligible. Sitting by Miguel's bed, holding his hand and stroking his brow, all I could do was speak to him in my heart. His wife told me that sometimes he would come stumbling home, sobbing that he was too drunk to pray and asking her to pray to Jesus for him. I silently told him that it was now time to ever so gently let go of the suffering of this life and go on to the Jesus he loved so much. From my heart, I told him, "This life of pain is closing behind you now. Let it go. Your work in this life is about done. All you need to do now is move toward the light streaming from His sacred heart."

Feeling after an hour or so that I had done all I might under the circumstances, I took my leave. Standing in the hallway, catching my breath and considering who I was supposed to see next, Miguel's wife came out and asked me to return because "Miguel said he would like you there."

I spoke to him in my heart of softening to the pain and having faith in the compassion that awaited him. He quieted considerably, and just before he settled into death, quite to everyone's surprise, he sat up in bed and said, "*La luz, la luz*" ("The light, the light"). Though we did not speak the same language, the heart needs no translation.

It is impossible to measure what use this heart speech might be to one who has died, but it seems of considerable value to the sender of such wholehearted blessings. A former teacher of mine who died years ago felt completely lost to me until gradually, even with a smile at times, I came to realize and enjoy a certain irony: in those last years, he was at times difficult to get in touch with, and we exchanged weeks of phone tag before we made contact; yet, of late I could get him on the—pardon the expression—"heartline" anytime I wished. We speak more often now than ever. His guidance is even more precious.

We meet most directly in the heart.

I have on occasion speculated whether those who have died, finding themselves "in a better place," experience their version of survivor's sorrow watching their loved ones grieve.

And what of that experience when the recently departed seem somehow to return momentarily, always with that same message, "I'm okay, everything is okay," in whatever belief system one has?

I wonder sometimes when the living experience an apparition of a departed loved one whether one's departed might be dreaming of them, just as they are dreaming of the other, and somehow pass through that same portal for a moment to show that the heart connection is never lost.

Send blessings for well-being to a departed loved one. Remind them of their capacity for mercy. Tell them to forgive themselves as you forgive them. Feel how the pain of separation and the helplessness it entails no longer predominate, how "there is something I can do now to connect, through my love for that loved one, back to myself." And perhaps in our silent heart speech, having ourselves broken loose of some of the dark fantasies of Judgment Day, we envision what a gentle, forgiving afterworld might be like. Encourage them, though they may still be drawn by the grief-intensified love of their family, friends, and lovers, to let go and go on, to trust their rapidly intensifying inner light and follow it to the essence of wisdom and love itself. Part of finishing your business is encouraging them to finish their business.

As the past fades into the present, instead of intensifying a feeling of helplessness, say to your loved one something like, "Go into the perfect possibilities of what awaits you. All the 'I could haves' and 'should haves' are all done now. If there ever was a time to let go into the present, this is it." Know that you are not abandoning but encouraging them; tell them you love them and will miss them but now it is their time to shine.

In the wake of the loss of a loved one, there may be an involuntary cramping of the mind that perhaps only the heart can release with a profound and loving "good-bye," a good-bye that remembers that the origin of the phrase is "God be with you." Words that sear the lips but relieve the heart. A "sending off" that is at first sour on the tongue but gradually becomes sweet. At first so dominated by loss, at last so connected by love. A farewell that allows the continuation of life on the terms given. It is not a putting of that person out of the heart but rather inviting them to settle within, beyond the compulsive grasping of the mind. To let them *be* as they are, as they must.

14

MAKING PEACE
WITH OUR SORROW

THERE ARE THREE STAGES TO WORKING WITH MENTAL
AND PHYSICAL SORROW.

The first stage is softening to the pain. Unattended sorrow becomes
embedded in the mind and body. Identify your area of discomfort.
Locate the sensations associated with your state of mind, what some
call the "feeling of feelings." Explore the physical characteristics of afflictive mental states, in what is called the body pattern of grief. Note
the hardness in your belly, the tightness in your jaw, the contraction
around your breath, and begin to soften to the hardness and the tension
in those areas.

The art and science of softening is cultivated, first and best, in the soft belly practice. Let go of the holding and the hardness that reside in your abdomen with each successively softer breath. Soften the flesh, the tissue, and the muscle; even soften into the marrow, letting go of the grief-holding over a lifetime. Discover the power of level after level of softening that can be sent into any area of your mind or body that calls for peace. Open the area to the infiltration of a healing mercy.

The second stage is the cultivation of mercy.

As the sensations of sorrow in the mind and/or body are met with something softer than aversion and a tendency to abandon anything unpleasant, the physical sensation of softening will resonate with its mental counterpart of mercy, of kindness where kindness was rarely considered before. It's an opening of the fist that grasps the pain, exposing it to a willingness to let love in. As absurd, challenging, and exciting as it sounds, we begin to send loving kindness into those parts of ourselves abandoned to hopelessness and fear. We start to flood the area once filled with the hatred for our pain with a soothing, cooling kindness. We are not "loving our pain," as some might fear; we are sending love to ourselves *even though we are in pain.* We are not putting ourselves out of our hearts just because we are not the way we wish to be.

Mercy is cultivated first and best in the practice of forgiveness, compassion, and loving kindness meditations. Just as the softness that's cultivated in the belly is transferable to any part of the body and becomes gradually more capable of releasing the mental tension manifest in its body pattern, so too does the mercy accumulated in forgiveness and acts of kindness and service to others become available to settle those afflictive states of mind.

The last stage of working with mental and physical sorrow involves making peace with it.

Here I am not speaking of enlightenment but simply "lightenment," the incremental letting go of suffering. Make peace with your sorrow. Encourage yourself toward forgiveness and gratitude for even the hard lessons you've had to learn and thankfulness for the path that leads toward peace.

To have closure is to make peace with your pain. To integrate your pain into your heart is to make peace with the warring factions within.

This warring is inner conflict. Grief is war, a sense of defeat. Most of the qualities that make up grief, both immediate and long lasting, are at war. Denial is at war. Resistance is at war. Bargaining is at war. Anger is at war. Doubt is at war. Fear is endlessly at war, as are judgment, guilt, and shame. Distrust, helplessness, hopelessness: *War!* The stress-fatigue that buries us in unhallowed ground leaves us chronically war-weary and torn of heart. War is liking this and disliking that, from moment to moment all day long. Superiority is war. Inferiority is war. In the world within and around us, heaven and hell are constantly warring for our approval. The war-torn heart longs for a moment's peace.

The less we make peace with our pain, the more we tend to make war on others.

Unattended sorrow degrades whole cultures that insist on the suppression of painful feelings. It creates a cultural ennui, a thinly disguised foreboding that slowly sublimates into a materialism capable of destroying the spirit of most religions. It's a melancholy that atrophies nerve endings, making it difficult to touch or feel. It's an underlying disquiet and dissatisfaction.

The more we leave a person, or persons, alone with their pain, without recourse to mercy or mutual concern for each other's wellbeing, the more withdrawn and narcissistic as a society we become. And the more able to violate another human being because, numb with underlying grief, we give little attention to the outcome of our actions.

This cultural numbing creates a politically infantile worldview that can't see beyond its own immediate needs nor comprehend that anyone else feels pain as much as we do. It reinforces the least in us. It forgets itself in violence to ourselves and to others, and sours our worldview. Its legacy, from generation to generation, is the war-torn heart. It abandons its veterans, giving them shamefully inadequate support and care. It makes big war but has little idea of how to serve the peace. It casts a cold eye on its most heroic servants. It leaves its dead on the battlefield.

Alex, once perpetually sad and sleep-deprived, without many meaningful relationships and torn by war, said,

"My oldest brother was killed in Vietnam when I was quite young. My parents didn't know what to do with their feelings and stuffed them down. It deadened the house. Vietnam was what they called 'an unpopular war,' and you were very unpopular for dying in it. We didn't have anything in terms of community support. My parents were supposed to just somehow go on with their lives as if nothing had happened.

"So in their trying to protect each other from the family pain, they left me to figure out for myself how not to drown. I had to cry into my pillow. I had to find a friend to talk to, and I don't know how I would have gotten through it without her. I still thank her, wherever she is, in my prayers.

"How grateful I am that I learned to deal more directly with my sorrow, by talking about it with others who also had great losses, because I lost my son a year and a half ago and sought and received tremendous support since then. Having learned over the previous years how to allow those feelings to the surface, I can now allow these feelings—the anger, frustration, and even the feeling of being cheated—to be said out loud.

"It's very easy to deceive yourself and deceive society and have everyone think you're okay when you're not. It's so important for me personally to keep taking care of myself and grieve when I need to grieve and enjoy myself when I can without feeling guilty for not feeling worse."

Alex might be said to be in something of a "successful grief," one that can look into itself, and attend to itself, with mercy. He can be in pain without closing his heart to himself. He's not "cured," but his world is expanded a bit. He can sleep at night, and he can "even care again sometimes."

Wars are rarely fought by those who have anything to gain but by those who have everything to lose. The private in any army often has more in common with his opposing counterpart looking down a rifle barrel at him than with his own officers.

We have become so adept in the justifications for the slaying of so many parts of ourselves that it takes but a wobbling leap of faithlessness to open the bomb-bay doors and pull the lever that kills the rest of us. Discoveries in brain science indicate that aversion and anger come from the rear of the brain, while peace and the calming, appreciative qualities arise in the frontal lobes that come together like hands in prayer. It may well be said, then, that we make war in the back of our brains and make peace just behind the brow. We often have war in the back of our mind. And we make peace when we put our brows together to see through another's eyes, looking toward the end of conflict within and around us. But when trauma swells the adrenal cortex and fear shrinks the frontal lobes to a fist, we become angry and alternately numb and hypersensitive, full of blame and remorse, frozen at the edge of life.

When our unspoken grief, our unattended sorrow, becomes the common treaty where no one crosses the line of impropriety by speaking of the dead within us, we forget the song of peace and even sing patriotically, ethnocentrically, of war. We declare it is "the others" that are the cause of our lack of peace and must pay the price for our embarrassment and dismay.

To find peace, we must enter the pain that if left unattended leads to suffering. We must settle the war of the worlds battling within us.

The less we are able to soften to fear and grief, the less we are able to meet ourselves or others with compassion or see our way to peace. Opening to our pain, we recognize the pain we all share and become more able to relate to the suffering of others.

If we wish to make peace in this world, we must recognize the causes of suffering and follow the pain, the pain we all share, to the shared heart.

For years, Ondrea and I spoke to groups about the classically eccentric Zen master Paul Reps and when he was attempting to visit some of his teachers in Japan in the 1950s. He was turned away by an Asian immigration officer who said that since Japan was being used as a staging area for the war in Korea, his visit was not allowed because it was not "militarily allied." Turning over the rejected immigration form, Reps wrote on the back, "Making a cup of green tea I stop the war." He handed it back to the government official, who looked at what had been written and initialed approval of the visa, looking up to say, "We need more people like you in our country right now."

Reps, it seems, was referring to the harmony that is possible between man and his environment, even between nations and individuals, the peace that might be found in the clear presence displayed in even the mindful preparation of a cup of tea: the melody of the splash of cold water pouring from the faucet; the subtle sounds of the slowly rising bubbles in the kettle. Not the impatient waiting that creates anxiety and opposition; just being. Living quietly in the body that feels the cold cup in its hand gradually warming to its touch. Experiencing the fragrance of green tea, not thinking "tea" or imagining its taste, but just whole-heartedly present for the process. Sitting down quietly and sipping at peace, mind nowhere else but in the heart of the matter. Making a cup, drinking a cup in a sacred manner, we stop the war.

Being so thoroughly present in everyday activities, we make peace with each intention, each sensation, each state of mind, as it arises and passes away. Even conflicting opinions meet equal-mindedly before they begin to war. Before anger and guilt, confusion and denial, turn violent.

First we need to learn to make peace with a cup of tea, then we can lay down our weapons of self-destruction and meet with mercy our fears in another's eyes across the table.

I've shared this process of peacemaking, in a good deal more detail, for years with various groups. One day during a workshop, as I walked from the auditorium after we broke for lunch, a fellow supported by a walker came slowly down the center aisle toward me. He had obviously been ill for some time, his body thinned to a near skeletal form. When we met, he looked up at me with sparkling eyes and said, "Dying of cancer I stop the war." We stood together in an ocean of peace as people streamed noisily by on their way to lunch, on their way to a cup of tea, on their way to war or peace. He wasn't backing away from cancer or anything else in his life. He was, as they say, present and accounted for. Peace emanated from him.

He said pain had taught him that the heart was his only refuge. He said years of jockeying for position in the academic world, of struggling with cancer and the loss of his dear wife, of being bedridden with pain, of fighting *with* life in the guise of fighting *for* life had burned through his long-conditioned desire to stay hidden and safe. He said it had drawn him out of the closet of his life into a world of boundless being. "Dying of cancer I stop the war."

Entering wholeheartedly into our fear, our anger, we stop the war.

Life sings again and again that peace comes from mercy and violence from isolation, and that the more we are able to receive our pain with kindness, the more likely we are to offer these conditions to another.

Making peace with our common grief we stop the war.

15

WHAT IS THE BODY PATTERN OF GRIEF?

WHAT DOES FEAR BORN OF SORROW FEEL LIKE IN THE BODY? As with all afflictive emotional states, disturbing states of mind that assail the heart with guilt and judgment and tighten the belly with anger and fear, it is often easier to relate to them first as their patterns within the body: the tightness in the jaw or gut as the body contracts around feelings of helplessness and hopelessness, all the loss that has retreated into our eyes and bones. Recognizing the body patterns of grief, we can learn to soften to that tension instead of feeling defeated by the idea that fear and anger are our only alternatives.

Indeed, when we live aware in our body, sometimes a stiffness in the back of the neck or a hardening in the belly will foretell the state of mind that is just about to poke its head into ours.

One of the results of looking into the sensations that accompany afflictive states can at first be to discover that you can't feel much at all. In the throes of acute grief we can barely feel our body. We are deadened. We seem to keep bumping into things. We can barely taste our food or see a sunset. What used to give us pleasure now holds none. The mirrors of our heart are draped in sackcloth. Familiar music drains our spirit.

It infiltrates our daily experience. Our resistance to life as it slips beyond our control is evident in the body. It presents itself as that soreness in the lower back, or the anxiety in the tongue that's been held stiff to guard against letting too much slip past.

The closing down of the senses in the absence of a loved one, or the loss of love itself, can also be experienced by some people as a sense of our own absence—the departure of not only another's life force but our own. It's a sense of powerlessness to control what comes next, a loss of self. It's a feeling, as one person put it, that "I am living someone else's life in someone else's body."

What might it be like to devote a liberating awareness to investigating the pathways grief takes within the body, instead of turning away from them?

We can most easily approach afflictive emotional states through how they express themselves in the body. They are stabilized when we turn an increasing focus on the field of sensation, and we are less liable to be seduced by the thoughts that make painful feelings seem less vulnerable to exploration than they actually are.

To approach our afflictive emotional states, we need to find where loss is stored in the body.

There's a considerable amount of grief that becomes sequestered in the body. Sorrow filters through every sense we have—the eyes, the ears, the nose, even the skin. We experience unattended sorrow's deep penetration into the mind.

Buddha once gave a talk called the fire sermon. He said the eyes are on fire. The ears are on fire. The nose is on fire. The tongue is on fire. The body is on fire. The mind is on fire. The sense doors are ablaze with desire and disappointment.

It's hard to hold our pain in and still pretend we're not on fire.

Indeed, this is true even of those "with no discernable grief," those with only the common frustration and dissatisfaction of ordinary grief. Most people who come to me and say they've "got their shit together" are actually standing in it at the time.

When we open our heart to our pain, we make it safe for life to re-inhabit our body.

Not waiting for our healing to appear out of thin air, we go looking for it ourselves; the investigation begins in the marrow.

TRACKING SORROW
THROUGH THE BODY

When we relate to an afflictive emotion such as fear instead of reacting to it, we start to reinhabit our body.

Note how each state of mind has its own personality, and listen mercifully to the content, even the tone of voice. How is it affecting the rhythm of the breath? What is its choice of language? What happens to our thoughts when, instead of meeting them with fear, we allow them to come and go without comment?

What does it feel like to settle back in the flow of consciousness and watch fear float harmlessly by? How remarkably freeing! Nothing is too good to be true.

When we meet fear with kindness, a forgotten satisfaction arises as the energy we've been using to hold it back is released.

We think we have a handle on what grief is until someone asks a seemingly innocuous question, such as, "Is there more sensation on the right or left side of your body?" Only then do we find that we don't know what's happening behind our eyes, or what's happening behind our right ear or under the skin of our left hand.

This grief has arisen so many times, but we still find it difficult to answer specific questions about the experience of anger, or any other heavy emotion, because we have always attempted to elude our pain.

Where's your tongue when you're angry? Is it curled against the roof of your mouth? Against your front teeth? Is it pressed against the floor of your mouth? Is your body slowly turning to stone? What's happening in your gut? What do you feel in the soles of your feet? Can you still feel the earth, or is there just a dull pressure against this body you sometimes feel painfully locked into? What's going on behind your left knee? What are you experiencing in your spine, in your lower back, in your sphincter?

And what happens when you soften around pain, simply allowing it to be there without the resistance that turns it to suffering? What happens when mercy infiltrates your wounds? What happens when it permeates those parts of yourself you have abandoned in fear and loathing?

We have run away from most of our pain for so long that we now have no idea how to deal with it. But when we allow the heart to stay open to the emotional unfolding, instead of the mind closing around it, we are less afflicted by the not unexpected occasional reappearance of such feelings. We begin to experience a healing that breaks our habitual withdrawal from pain and from life itself.

16

REENTERING
THE BODY

GRIEF IS OFTEN, IN THE LEAST PRODUCTIVE MANNER, an out-of-body experience. The accumulation of unattended sorrow belabors our thoughts and emotions and numbs us to our deepest workings so that we hardly feel ourselves present any longer, seemingly displacing us from our body.

Soften the belly and feel this body you were born into. Allow awareness to enter into the fields of sensation by which you know you are alive, and feel the sensations of being in that body: warmth and coolness, pressure on the bottoms of your feet when you are standing and on the buttocks when you are sitting, the full range of muscle extensions and contractions when you rise from a chair or your bed, the movement in the chest and belly with each breath.

Awareness is life itself; *where our attention is, we are most alive.* Feel life in the body, in the mind, and let it all be received in the heart that's so capable of love.

When we cultivate a soft belly, we can expand the practice into a body-sweeping meditation, focusing an ever-softening merciful awareness as it slowly sweeps through the sensations generated in the body, from the top of the head to the bottoms of the feet.

Bring your attention to the top of your head until you pick up whatever sensations are there. As you quiet yourself, you can begin to feel the difference between your scalp and your skull. You can almost feel where they meet. Then, soften to receive the sensations in your brow, moving slowly down your face to feel the sides of your head, the bridge of your nose, your nostrils, lips, tongue, and mouth. Gradually, let awareness sweep into your body through the sensations in your neck, perhaps going from vertebra to vertebra. Feel down each arm, focusing awareness as it passes from finger to finger.

Take your time, noting the areas here and there that have more sensation than others. Soften to those areas as you go.

Continue through the torso, through the levels of heart and belly, hard and soft, down through the legs. Let the energy of awareness proceed through your knees and into your feet, and feel it move from toe to toe, reuniting with the ground beneath.

Slowly sweep through your body, receiving sensations as they arise from your muscles, tissue, and flesh. Feel your body fill with life awareness. Stop anywhere there is stronger sensation, pain, or stiffness to examine the moment-to-moment changes there. Make peace with the old wars in your body. Send mercy into lost blessings. Reenter your body with mercy, or, as some might say, "continue on with your birth."

Send a healing loving kindness through your body, filling it as if it were the body of the world itself.

Now, send mercy to all those people who are working with this same grief, this same sense of loss, at this same moment. Embrace the community of sorrow with loving kindness so that it is not just your grief but the grief of all those who too are bent by loss. It is not just our isolated healing but the healing of everyone who is so confused by uncontrollable impermanence. Let this be our conspiracy of healing—a conspiracy of the shared heart.

17

ATTENDING THE MINDSET OF LOSS

GRIEF DOES NOT SO MUCH END AS IT DOES CHANGE IN INTENSITY AND DURATION.

Our states of mind are constantly in flux, be they unpredictable sorrow, fear, love, sweet remembrance, loss, or helplessness. Uninvited sorrow cries itself to sleep.

We rarely know all that we feel. States of mind arise uninvited, while random thoughts speak their mind. When we investigate our feelings instead of blindly following them, relating to them with mercy and mindfulness instead of only relating from them with fear and despair, we can glimpse the difference between freedom and bondage.

Investigation is a prime example of relating to a feeling or state of mind: noting its changing realities, how it feels in the body, how it keeps changing, "going through changes" in the mind, as it weaves through its constituent states, observing the fear, the doubt, the expectation, the disappointment, et cetera, that compose it, watching how fear may stimulate it and how mercy may pacify it.

To cross the barriers to the heart, we need to take some time away from the madding crowd, or the maddening absence of any companionship at all, to explore the qualities of thought that are most clearly affected by loss.

Anger, fear, doubt, sadness—all emotions, oppressive or otherwise—are a *process*, not a single state of mind. They are composed of constantly changing individual emotions. For instance, if we observe anger, which we've always believed to be a single state of mind, we find that it turns out to be a multileveled process: a moment of blocked wanting, of dissatisfaction, followed by a moment of frustration, followed by a rapid unfolding and looplike return through fear and pride and doubt and judgment and distrust, alternately shadowboxing and finger-pointing, merciless with the world and with ourselves.

Grief and all the afflictive emotions that are associated with it have a certain hallucinatory quality about them that insists it is going to go on forever and only going to get worse. All afflictive states hold this false promise of unending difficulty. Yet no state of mind is not impermanent: no hate that cannot be displaced by loving kindness, no fear than cannot be displaced by courage, no ignorance that cannot be uprooted by insight. Fear says, "I will ruin you!" and a moment later, turning toward fear with mindful fascination, we find ourselves "a whole new person." But there is a way to stay present with the delusion of permanence in the essentially impermanent world without closing around it.

Grief is a great intensifier of doubt, of distrust in our life being anything other than in the pain it now finds itself. Exploring doubt—that pushing away of alternatives, investigating the long dark halls of its labyrinthine sense of loss of confidence in anything new—we are able to palpate its inner nature, its constituent characteristics of fear in all its flourish and disguise, such as resistance, skepticism, suspicion, incredulity, paranoia, indecision, and inferiority in the very texture of doubt. We find ourselves relating to doubt or dismay rather than feeling isolated and alone, doubting all we see and hear from it and in so doing find our identification with that state of mind greatly diminished. Even the seemingly dead zone of cold indifference we find can be entered when mercy and forgiveness are focused within it in kind investigation.

Watching the process of our grief as it manifests in the body and mind, we find a diminishment of our latent sorrow as we wrestle our way through it and note that each withdrawal from its effects, each attempt to numb our grief, turns our belly to fire and stone.

We begin to discover just how much of our anger, our fear, and our distrust in everything but our pain is a manifestation of unattended sorrow. Every instance of feeling unsafe, every moment of doubt or shame, each afflictive emotion arises like a billow of smoke from a fire we fear can never be extinguished.

Unresolved grief results from not only the loss of a loved one but also from the way that life roller-coasters between clinging for dear life and a hollowness in the pit of the stomach.

Most of our resentments in life, no matter how guilefully disguised by the mind, are actually a grief reaction spawned from earlier feelings of loss. Most feelings of aversion—most of those feelings of being ill at ease, of doubt, and of unwillingness to go further—are conditioned, even habituated, by a previous sense of safety lost. Indeed, we can see that even our tendency to judge others is an aspect of grief: a feeling of "not-enoughness," which we long to be otherwise. Every moment of jealousy, confusion, or hatred arises from the belly of sorrow.

Though our various levels of grief may try to persuade us that it is fruitless, our healing lies in nonetheless allowing a merciful awareness to sink through the layers of our grief and explore what might lie beyond our pain. It may take being lost in the maze of feeling totally hopeless and helpless before we can eventually surrender our pain, open it to investigation and eventual healing. But what else can we do?

What lies beyond the disquiet of simultaneously clinging to and condemning life is the spaciousness of the heart that becomes uncovered by a liberating awareness.

As we explore the path toward the heart, we might discover that the moment-to-moment investigation of emotions—even dissatisfaction—can be very satisfactory. We reverse the gravity of heavy states of mind by noting their constituent elements. As we move from the obvious to the subtle, the easier, the lighter the emotions become. It's relating to "just this much" at a time, as in watching individual snowflakes instead of trying to stop the storm. We do not become snow-blind; we are strengthened rather than weakened.

In the direct examination of even such afflictive emotions as helplessness, there arises a sense of empowerment. As we investigate our wounding, penetrating the phalanxes of fear that in confusion attempt to protect our pain, we begin to recognize that emotion in its moment-to-moment unfolding as a process, not just some immovable monolith. We begin to note the unfolding into the familiar echoes of hopeless fear, self-distrust, muffled anger, and the desire to just give up and die. If we watched this process as though it were occurring in a mourning child, we could not but weep for its suffering as it holds a mirror of mercy up to our pain, unrecognized compassion rising even for so unlikely a soul as ourselves, reawakening trust in our healing potential.

It isn't sadness or anger or guilt that limits our access to the heart; it's our negative attachment to these emotions, our intense wish for them to be otherwise, our dark dance with them But by moving toward these feelings we have always pulled away from and exploring them moment by moment, heartbeat to heartbeat, breath by breath, we come to see clearly their inner nature.

Fortunately for all of us, we are able to cultivate much of this healing in practices that revive the heart and recover the spirit. The Zen master cries when she is sad and laughs when she is joyful. Being fully alive, nothing is denied and nothing is left incomplete. It is her sworn duty to be so fully in the present that thoughts of the past and dreams of the future flow equally through her heart, never denying that letting go of our suffering is the hardest work we will ever do.

We have been using up so much of our life energy just to get by that when that holding to our suffering, our considerable identification with our grief, is somewhat relieved, there is an energy released that would be difficult to differentiate from joy. And we see a way through, after all.

When we investigate, we find beneath the grief of anger a reservoir of sadness. And beneath that sadness, an ocean of love beyond our wildest dreams.

18

A DAY OF WALKING

AFTER THE OPENINGS TO SUCH DEEP FEELINGS AS THE PRECEDING CHAPTERS encourage, it is time to consider taking not a day off but—if I may—a "day in." The empirical "days" chapters— walking, practicing loving kindness, making peace with pain, silence, forgiveness, singing, compassion, and love—are experiments in healing. Woven throughout the book, they are "focus days" in which powerful mental states and the deeply embracing characteristics of the heart are emphasized and further cultivated. Today, take yourself for a walk.

Walking, much like singing, steadies the mind. When we place one foot in front of the other, we can feel the body lean and sway as we move forward. The first steps may be slow, but gradually we find our gait. Though we may require effort to break our inertia, our willingness to move is soon requited. At first, we find the mind doing the walking; then the body soon takes over, and with that, our thoughts are free to flow.

With each step, as the mind gradually begins to note the sensations in each footfall, we reenter and become present in our body. We can feel the muscles lift the foot, swing it forward, then place it back on the ground, noting the moment when both feet touch the earth before the next foot rises to the challenge. When we attend to the moment-by-moment sensations that accompany each step, it is as though we are learning to walk all over again. We can imagine what it must have been like to take our first steps as a toddler. It's a sense of accomplishment and freedom rarely rivaled in the years that follow.

Just as we experience the field of sensation when we walk, awareness of our thoughts also becomes more precise. As we watch the beginning, the middle, and the end of each step, perhaps we notice thoughts with that same focused attention—the beginning, middle, and end of each thought—before each blends into the next. As our focus sharpens, we may for an instant see the spacious awareness that equally buoys our joy and our sorrow.

After walking for a while, stop to rest in the dappled shadow of an ample tree. Sit quietly, reflecting with the mindfulness accumulated with each step fully noticed. Feel the body you sit in, listen for the sounds that take a moment to hear, feel the air on your skin, watch thoughts roll by like boxcars at a railroad crossing, view the mind's ever-changing content as a process, the unfolding, of the passing show. Feel how hard the belly has become from fruitlessly attempting to protect itself from pain, and allow a little more mercy into this storehouse of grief.

As we become more observant of our surroundings, we become more aware of our inner habitat as well. Slowly, what was hidden becomes visible: an ant purposefully scouting for the tribe, a bee testing pollen, clouds that remind us of elephants and fallen friends. Gradually, what was unheard begins to resonate in the inner ear again: birdsongs varying, the wind singing differently in the treetops than against the ground. A long, unrecalled memory appears, a love or pain forgotten, a moment of fear, a moment of anger, a moment of bewilderment, a moment of renewal passes behind the brow and through the heart. Settling through levels and levels of quiet, we cultivate the "warmth and patience breath." Breathing warmth and mercy into the heart center and slowly, patiently breathing out the holding, forgetfulness, and mercilessness that cast long shadows in the mind.

In fortunate moments, life becomes startlingly simple. There is no waiting for God or liberation. We rest in patience and watch how the heart at rest has room for all of creation. When we surrender our impatience, we can at last glimpse something too beautiful for words in what is around and within us: the sun illuminating the broad sky from horizon to horizon, and to our inherent radiance, the life-spark of awareness, illuminating the boundless mind.

Though we may sometimes walk to merely carry ourselves forward, at other times we might walk for the benefit of another person. Hiking with a child, as with any loved one, often opens new territory and reveals what has remained static within. Walking with a grieving child is a very skillful means of sharing thoughts and feelings. The conversation flows more easily, feelings are more readily expressed, and dreams are best recalled. Silence punctuates the forward movement in which each foot pauses to test the ground ahead.

I remember, once, walking for a long time through the vacuum created by the absence of a loved one. At first, my weeping and strong desire to turn around slowed my steps. But I walked through the wall of resistance as I continued talking to my dear one in my heart. Eventually, the loneliness, the unfinished business, and the remorse caused me to sit, trembling, by the path as long-forgotten memories came flooding into the astounding capacity of my heart. I delighted that so great a chasm of loss could coincide with a feeling of love so great that it soothed my broken world.

When we take one step after another, though at times we might fear becoming lost, we will eventually find our way home.

19

HEART BREATH

LILY HAD BEEN DEPRESSED FOR SOME TIME WHEN ONE EVENING, as she noticed the subtle nausea that often precedes an episode of grief, her attention was drawn into the ache growing at the center of her chest. The pain grew so great she couldn't breathe. It felt like her breath, maybe even her heart, might stop.

It seemed a very long time between breaths. Until she intuited, perhaps from a thousand incarnations of love and loss dormant in her cells, how a breath drawn directly into that ache can revive the heart.

Feeling there was some healing in the unusual intensity of this experience, sensing she might quench all this "fire eating," as she called it, she let go into it and let her breath disappear into her heart point.

Gasping for air like someone just pulled from the sea, she felt her chest burst open as she gratefully took a breath directly into her broken heart.

She felt her body shudder as a wave of mercy swept through her. And with a great sigh of relief, she began to breathe in all the love she had known in her life and began to breathe out some of the sorrow.

All that she had ever lost, all the grief buried over a lifetime, connected her with all the love that had been denied and the boon of compassion beneath her sorrow.

Although we have spoken of "opening the heart" as expanding into a state of mind, it can also refer to working with the energy center in the middle of the chest. Many yoga practices refer to this, which can be "opened" by various techniques that result in the experience of this spacious loving kindness. Though often blocked by unattended sorrow, the heart, when opened, creates a considerable release of energy and a very compassionate state of mind. The ancient practice of breathing into the energy center of the heart point can open a direct conduit to "our true heart."

When we are breathing into and out of the heart, venting it to the surface, the heart breathes deeper. Our life reaches all the way into what makes it precious. We can feel life expanding in the chest like a mother's arms opening to receive a new child. And when the heart expands to receive this new life, it is bigger than before because it has had to incorporate so much pain.

When there is a sense of loss, that very tender heart point becomes the grief point, which, for most people, is at least somewhat clogged by unresolved sorrow, disappointment, and a long-delayed disquiet begging for peace.

At the center of our chest we can feel something inspired by the origin of life itself: all of life and death, all of gain and loss, all of the miracles that we find beyond our fear and unfortunate attachment to our suffering.

When we peel back the layers of our sorrow, we find that another level of our life appears. Though it may seem at times that it is going to take a lifetime to penetrate unresolved grief, the feeling of being lost is slowly integrated, heart and soul, into a sense of new possibilities.

Out of the flurry of thoughts, sensations, and feelings, we begin to both feel the density that obscures our life and sense the aliveness just beyond it. These blockages of the pathway to the heart are hindrances to personal peace and universal compassion. It's a crown of thorns encircling the sacred heart.

In the grief point, our mental pain becomes a tangible and physical discomfort. Breathing into that ache at the center of the chest accesses the unattended sorrow as the grief point is slowly cleared of its blockages with a merciful breath and a mind that even forgives its pain opening the doorway known as "the touch point of the heart."

When we note that ache as the sad armoring over the heart, we can then breathe through to the ocean of compassion beneath that armor plating. Mercy penetrates layer after layer of fear and disappointment that blocks the entrance to the heart. Each layer is bound to the last by unattended sorrow.

When we surrender the rigidity that holds our suffering in place, mercy draws the pain out like a poultice. Mercy infiltrates between the layers once so isolated. When we meet the pain with a kindness that we have long lost confidence in, the cramping around the heart begins to loosen.

No longer losing our bearings in what once may have seemed the dark night of the soul, guided by the emanations of compassion through realms of gratitude and forgiveness once buried beneath so much sorrow, the unobstructed breath opens a passageway through strata after strata of consciousness, resuscitating the heart.

Lily, catching her breath, said,

"Breathing in mercy and forgiveness, I felt my heart begin to warm. Letting my breath, my life, go back out into the world, exhaling ever so slowly, it felt like a steel band was released from around my heart."

When we relinquish control of our breath, the breath breathes itself. We don't shape it or hold on to it. We let go of our lack of faith in the next breath and instead trust it to come on its own. When we let go of the distrust that girds the belly and extends even into the next breath, we allow the breath come and go in peace, softening to receive the rest of our life. No one ever dies from not breathing. We die when the heart stops.

20

TAPPING
THE RESOURCES
OF THE HEART

SOME OF THOSE WHO ARE BREATHING INTO THE HEART
also lightly tap on the grief point, as if gently waking a sleeping loved
one.

Many people find that a simple physical tapping of the grief point
produces a balance of energy in this area of the chest that encourages a
deeper surrender into compassion. There evolves an increasing trust in
the process.

Some people lightly tap the touch point of the heart in harmony with their breath or in rhythm with their walking in order to call the heart out of the shadows and aid us in our time of need.

In Japanese tradition, when a loved one dies, the mourners often wear white and shave their heads. Everyone in the community recognizes this gesture of love and joins in their prayer as they pass on the road. Perhaps one day we may see people tapping their hearts in rhythm with their steps as they walk down the street, and our community will be so connected that it awakens together, tapping for the good of the whole as they pass.

Tapping the heart is a powerful technique for getting through levels of numbness and unfinished business; it draws awareness and, thus, healing into that area. It encourages a merciful connection with the blockages to the heart, a shedding of our slowly accumulated armoring composed of layer after layer of disappointment and unresolved vulnerabilities.

Many people walk around most of their lives with holes in the center of their chests. By tapping the heart, we harmonize with the rhythm of the universe.   ·

The area around the heart point may be numb. Numbness is not a sign of lack but, rather, of presence. Inside most numbness is a considerable amount of sensation. As the heart is retrieved, there may arise an increasing intensity of sensation in the grief point as it is slowly cleared by the heart breath and a tapping of resources to reveal the touch point of the heart.

As breathing into the heart and tapping the grief point awaken the touch point of the heart, some people expand the process into a more direct contact with this very sensitive area by pressing gently into the grief point with the thumb and making small circles over the heart. As you try it, massage the very sensitive grief point, mindful of any tendencies to rush the process by pushing too hard or using too much force, as force closes the heart.

Many people recount that massaging small circles over the grief point while processing or remembering love and loss seemed to heighten the process of integrating loss, and they felt a sense of mercy issuing forth from their fingertips, each slow circumscription initiating greater access to the heart point.

Inviting the breath into the grief point and breathing in the warmth of our intention to revive the heart, our longing for wholeness establishes a direct conduit inward.

We pass through so much fear, doubt, and distrust, not to mention all the hidden things we have felt for so long but that we've been unable to reveal. All the ways we put ourselves out of our heart, all the self-prosecution and ostracized shame that constrict around loss.

Letting loose of our holdings, we take one breath after another into our heart. We receive hopelessness and helplessness into the ocean of our compassion that lies within the heart point.

Then, when we take our hand away a sacred circle can still be felt circumscribing the heart.

Like these practices of tapping the grief point and breathing into the heart, life itself is an experiment in truth. We are not going to rid ourselves of all our griefs in a weekend, or maybe even in an incarnation, but we may become able to meet our pain with love. And that changes our world.

Such practices can be initiatory, opening us up to whole new possibilities, or they may seem to be going absolutely nowhere. In either case, honor yourself with these practices a bit more than restlessness might wish. Our usual disbelief that the Buddha could have been referring to us when he said we could find no one more deserving of love than ourselves is in itself a form of unattended sorrow of the unattended need to rediscover ourselves, that invites us to a slow minuet around heart center.

Make these practices your own. It's okay that it takes a while. We need time to heal, to complete our birth, to come back whole into our world.

21

A DAY OF
LOVING KINDNESS

WHAT MIGHT IT BE LIKE TO AWAKEN TO A DAY DEVOTED
TO LOVING KINDNESS?

Loving kindness is the quality, the state of mind, that most demonstrates access to the ease of mind and unitive consciousness of the open heart. It is the quality that most overcomes our fear, aggression, and cold indifference.

This quality of making peace where there might be war was clearly demonstrated to me recently in a dream. Just before I woke up, I saw a nemesis of old and hardened my belly to her approach, but as she passed, quite to my surprise she brushed my cheek with a loving hand, and I felt my belly release its fear and my heart open like a lotus.

Loving kindness is a liberating, nonjudgmental state of clarity that accesses the heart and calms the mind. It inhabits thoughts with grace and actions with mercy. It softens the deeply imprinted hurtful compulsions of our ordinary mind and offers other options. It lessens hard judgments and affirms a whole new level of responsibility. *It is recognizing that responsibility is the ability to respond instead of the necessity to react.*

The practice of loving kindness begins with a basic commitment to non-injury. Non-injury has a quality of respect for all life, which continually reminds us that injury to others or ourselves, by word, deed, or even thought, arises from our own suffering. It reminds us to be loving with everyone—including ourselves. We are so forgetful of our true selves that sometimes even those people who have taken a pledge of non-injury to all sentient beings may exclude themselves from the category of beings that are so much in need of realistic compassion.

It is a rational intention to cause no suffering and to send the blessing of loving kindness into the inescapable pain that the production of our food and so many other life-supporting products produces. It is supremely rational to eat and breathe with gratitude, to move through our cities and our forests with some inkling of what Native Americans refer to as "walking in a sacred manner." Take the day lightly.

Loving kindness teaches us that we can be loving to those we do not love—even to those we do not like.

Of course, it is easier to direct feelings of care and kindness to our loved ones and friends. Gradually, we can learn to expand that circle to include those we do not even know, bringing them to mind and directing toward them thoughts for their well-being. We might even use the traditional loving kindness phrase, "May you be free from suffering, may you be at peace."

Let loose the fear that limits the expression of your heart, the natural tendency toward care for other beings. Note also that just as you wish to be happy, so do all other beings.

Loving kindness offers an expanded context for our lives in which we might find that extending thoughts of loving kindness toward others— even those we might dislike—may be less difficult than turning such thoughts toward ourselves. Extending love to ourselves opens a much obstructed pathway to unconditional love for all sentient beings because if we can love ourselves, we can love anyone.

Look upon yourself as if you were your only child, call yourself by your own first name, and say, "May I be free of suffering, may I be at peace." Though these words may bounce off your heart as though it were made of stone when you first turn toward yourself, over time they will enter to a noticeably increased appreciation, even sensitivity, to kindness and forgiveness that will then extend back out into the world. As the saying goes, "What comes around goes around."

Just as we may feel the accumulating power of loving kindness when directed toward ourselves, others may feel something of that same blessing when we direct it toward them. This increasing of the power of loving kindness is the work and delight of a lifetime.

"May all sentient beings be liberated from suffering. May all beings, from those taking their first breath to those taking their last, at this very moment experience the greatness of their true heart. May they know the joy that is their birthright."

Some people naturally fear that opening their hearts may make them too gullible or susceptible to others' bad intentions or prey to those who might take advantage of them. This always brings to mind the story of a friend who, as she slowly drove down a street in India in an open vehicle one night, was surprised by a drunken thug who lunged from a dark doorway and threw himself on her. Luckily, a male companion had the presence of mind to toss the offender off her and speed on. When she returned to the meditation center where she was staying, she went to her teacher to ask what might have been the appropriate response to such an attack. He asked her if she had her umbrella with her at the time, to which she responded that she did. And her teacher said, "You should have taken your umbrella and with all the loving kindness in your heart beaten that fellow over the head!"

Though the cultivation of love may begin with a state of mind in the course of time, it becomes a state of Being.

22

TRUSTING
OUR PAIN

TO MAKE PEACE WITH OUR PAIN, WE MUST COME TO TRUST IT enough to be able to approach it without tightening our belly. First we need to soften to our pain and send mercy into it, then finally we can perhaps make peace with it. To reclaim our heart we need to forgive ourselves for being in so much pain.

Perhaps the most difficult of the balancing acts we learn is to trust our pain, to let the healing in. Pain is surrounded by and encapsulated in fear. We tend to send hatred into our pains, whether physical or mental. Pain angers, tightens, and becomes exacerbated at the approach of anything but pity. When we send fear into pain it produces a tight knot of self-pity, but when we send love into it, it produces a compassion transferable to all pain. Indeed, on that first influx of mercy that attends our softening around our pain, it might be noticed how we may even resist feeling better.

The way in which we treat our pain is a demonstration in how we treat ourselves. How we push pain away displays how we attempt to elude all unpleasant experiences.

We have in our belly the most remarkable feedback device as to when and to what degree we are holding back from life: observing the hardness in our belly gives insight into the hardness of the mind.

If we harden to our mental and physical pain, go to war with it, and generally try to overpower it, the pain will eat us alive. The suppressed fear in our unattended sorrow is attracted to pain the way infection settles into an open wound. This sorrowful fear can make us want to die. It collects around every pain, every illness. It is this encrustation of resistance that exhausts a sizable portion of pain medication before it can ever reach the knot of sensations. Keeping our sorrow submerged is exhausting. It leaves us sore to the bone.

When we are in mental or physical pain, we often hold our breath. If we surrender the breath, no longer holding to it or attempting to manage it but rather trusting it to breathe on its own, we can begin, in letting go of control, to learn to make peace with our pain.

CREATING REALITIES

One of the concepts that may cause us to bury our pain is the notion that we are the sole creator of our reality, and thus create our own suffering. This idea, though innocently induced, reinforces whatever tendency we might have to believe we deserve to suffer. We think that if we got ourselves into it and can't work ourselves out of it, then it demonstrates our original weakness that caused the pain. It is one of those ideas to which my teacher used to refer when he said, "If you think it's so then it's so; if you think it's not so, then not so." It takes neither nature nor happenstance into consideration.

We do not create our reality; we effect our reality. Indeed, we are not responsible *for* our pain; we are responsible *to* our pain. The first concept creates the antihealing quality of guilt. The second opens our heart to our pain. You might be thrown forward watching the evening news, only to find out within the hour that you have had a heart attack; your reality has changed. We begin to upbraid ourselves for our diet, for our lack of exercise, and for one hundred other possible insults to our ailing heart. With each self-condemnation there is a tightening, an increase in the problem, a distancing from the solution. We make war with our illness or injury. But when we sit quietly with it, sending mercy, even forgiveness, into our hurting, there is a softening, a settling down within it, and a sense of considerably greater peace. Taking responsibility is to change our lifestyle, not to cultivate healing-blocking, heart-clutching self-hatred. In letting go of our deeply conditioned refusal to open around pain, in softening around the pain, we let the healing in.

Though we do not, on the level to which this conceit refers, create our pain, we always have the option of taking the teaching in compassion that pain offers. It is a conflict of interest between the closed superficialities of the conditioned mind and the unconditional love of the open heart. And it goes further than that. In the denial of responsibility to their own pain, some people rationalize the abnegation of responsibility to others in pain. They do not respond to the pain of others because they quite mercilessly believe those others brought it on themselves, denying the responsibility to their own pain, just as they covertly judge themselves for doing the same This is very dangerous thinking. Some even deify pain, believing that the more we suffer, the better it is for our soul.

The teacher whom I mentioned earlier often warned against mistaking practice for theory, saying nowhere was the difference more distinct than in people's uniquely different approaches to great pain, particularly on the deathbed. He used to note that every once in a while, in scriptures from as widely diverse a metaphysics as Buddhism and Catholicism, there can be found an insistence on the threat of hellish retribution, unfortunate rebirth, et cetera, that we must suffer to be holy.

Pointing directly, he'd say, "Suffering is not holy," and none of the "superstition and ritual" the Buddha warned against can make it so!

Such theories, perhaps the product of a fear of Judgment Day, are not borne out in practice. Searching through the depth and breadth of consciousness, there is no agony-for-a-seat-in-heaven trade-off to be found. No such retributive mercilessness exists.

Suffering is not grace. Grace is our true nature.

The exaltation of suffering has become a priest-craft perversion of the teachings of so many great hearts, from Jesus to Buddha to Muhammad. Such thinking easily results in a leap of faithlessness that becomes, at the extreme of some religions, the notion that we were born for roasting in hell.

Those who speak of encountering a near-death experience say that in the moments following death—in the dropping away of pain and an attachment to the body—a feeling of delight arises that even the most austere holy books cannot deny is our true nature.

Taking my hand in his, my teacher reminded me that if we attend to our lives with loving kindness, if we make peace with our pain, our death will take care of itself.

23

A DAY IN THE HEART OF PAIN

WHAT WOULD IT BE LIKE TO AWAKEN TO A DAY WITH OUR HEARTS open to our pain?

What would it be like to approach the mean habit of rejecting our pain, which turns it into suffering, with mercy and awareness? When we are no longer mesmerized by our wounds or making a religion of the pain by which we so often define ourselves, we stop running for our lives.

Some years ago, sitting next to a fifteen-month-old child whose cancer had begun in her mother's womb, as I prayed for her life, something very deep inside told me to stop, that I didn't know enough to make such a prayer. It said that I was just second-guessing God. That I could not really comprehend what her spirit might have needed next, that only this pain in this fleeting body, which was being torn from the hearts of her loved ones, might teach her as she evolved toward her ceaseless potential. That she, like us all, was in the lap of the Mystery, and that the only appropriate prayer was, "May you get the most out of this possible!"

Sharing our healing, we send wishes for the well-being of all those who, like ourselves, find themselves in a difficult moment, as the heart whispers, "May we all get the most out of this possible."

And we can say to ourselves, in appreciation of the healing potential of approaching with mercy and awareness that which so recently may have been an aversion to our situation, "May I get the most out of this possible."

It is said that nothing is true until we have experienced it, so as an experiment in sending love where the fear is, we can use the presence of mild pain to test the truth of softening and sending mercy into an area of our body that is perhaps captured in the constriction of fear. Knowing that working with physical pain demonstrates a means of working with mental pain as well, we can let go of the tension around physical discomfort.

If you watch closely, you'll notice that when you experience physical pain, you ostracize and isolate that part of yourself. You close off what is calling out for your help. We do the same thing with our grief.

When you stub your toe, more than physical pain is generated; grief is released into the wound, followed by a litany of dissatisfactions and "poor me's," a damning of God sent heavenward. When we trip and fall in the darkness we are all too ready to curse ourselves for being so clumsy, as well as for not being able to hold our bladder until dawn, for not counting the hours in our just-expended 1,000-hour lightbulb, and the bruise is suffused with self-judgment and an irrational sense of responsibility.

The next time you have a minor wound, such as a stubbed toe or bumped elbow, note how long it takes that wound—when you soften to it and use it as a focus for loving kindness—to heal. Then compare it with the number of days it takes a similar wound to heal when you turn away from it, allowing the fear and resistance that rushes toward it to mercilessly remain. Contrast the healing of an injury in the mind or body in which loving kindness has gradually gathered to one that has been abandoned.

This softening and opening around pain has been shown in several double-blind studies to provide greater access of the immune system to an area of injury. It opens the vice of resistance into a never-considered acceptance of the moment. It denies hopelessness a home. It proves we are not helpless, that we can actively intercede in what we previously believed we had only to endure.

Working with our pain, or the pain of loved ones, cultivates a mercy that allows us to stay one more moment at their bedside when we are most needed. It allows us to not run away.

To open some of our healing potential, soften around the pain to melt the resistance that isolates it. Enter it with mercy, instead of walling it off with fear. Pass through the barricades of fear and distrust that attempt to defend the pain. Let what seems an improbable love—the ultimate acceptance of our pain—enter the cluster of sensations that so agitate the mind and body.

It takes patience to let go of doubt. So many fears warn us against opening beyond the numbness that surrounds pain. But when we allow ourselves to be open to and investigate these fears, we come to see them and our negative attachment to them, our compulsive warring with them, as a great unkindness to ourselves. As we open into our pain we may weep with gratitude when at last the pain does not so much disappear as become dispersed through the gradually expanding spaciousness of awareness.

As pain teaches us that fear can be penetrated by mercy and awareness, from some inherent knowing there resonates from our suffering a perfect teaching in compassion. We find in our pain the pain we all share. Softening around pain with mercy instead of hardening it with fear, the heart expands as "my" pain becomes "the" pain. Odd as it may sound, when we share the insights arising from *our* pain we become more able to honor *the* pain.

Following a tributary from the personal to the universal, we can find in *our* pain *the* pain of others as well. In our own wish to be free of suffering, others are calling out to be freed from their difficulties. Finding them in ourselves, the loving kindness that we extend to all sentient beings moves Earth toward heaven.

When we meet pain with mercy, there is a silent sigh of understanding and relief that can serve the whole world. There is exposed a meaning to life, a connection through ourselves to all others, that proposes a balm to the suffering in the world.

24

MINDFULNESS: AN INVITATION TO LIBERATION

MINDFULNESS IS KNOWING WHAT YOU ARE DOING WHILE YOU ARE DOING IT—experiencing your life not as an afterthought but as a *living presence*.

I marvel at the ability of consciousness to observe itself and the grace of our capacity to cultivate a liberating awareness of the passing show of consciousness. I am in awe of the faculty of "the watcher," the soul of mindfulness, to witness our life with kindness and clarity, without becoming lost in the commentary that floats by on the stream of consciousness. The capacity to simply note the "voices from other rooms" or images from the "family album" without getting lost in reverie or spinning out into the same old daydreams we have so often substituted for our daily life. Letting go of the irretrievable past and the unpredictable future, we discover our selves in the living present.

Watching the breath at the nostrils or in the softening belly, focusing on the moment-to-moment sensation that accompanies each inhalation and exhalation, we enter the present at the level of wordless sensation. Big quiet. Concentration gradually gathers in which no thought or sensation, memory or desire is pushed away but is noted with a choiceless awareness, a completely nonjudgmental openmindedness, that watches one thought melt into the next, one feeling after another present itself, tell its story, and move on. Though our restless conditioning may insist that just watching the unfolding will not be enough to overcome and break through our deep confusion and dissatisfactions, we find that nothing heals quite like awareness. Seeing clearly each thought as it arises against the silent background of the field of sensation, we watch the beginning, middle, and end of each thought and the space between, and the ongoing unfolding process of the mind and body.

As passive as this process of sharpening awareness to observe the flow of consciousness may seem, in actuality the content of the mind, from fear to greed, from doubt to hatred, is healed by the repeated touch of simple awareness.

Noting your feelings without judgment, labeling each state of mind as it arises, mentally differentiating each, such as fear, anger, doubt, or judgment, you continue to relate *to* the mind instead of *from* it. Recognize how these feelings, if allowed to continue in their own usual compulsive manner, leave us unremittingly afflicted by oppressive emotions.

In the stillness, the breath breathes itself in the momentary body as sensation after sensation, thought after thought passes through the increasing vastness of awareness. Watching the flow of consciousness, we see how easily we slip into identification with the passing dream and imagine ourselves so much smaller than we are, forgetting the deathless awareness that originally entered the body to produce life and forever survives death.

The more aware we are, the closer we are to love.

When the cold indifference with which we attempt to freeze our pain begins to melt, the heart becomes more fully alive.

As mindful exploration increases, so does the clarity of a strengthening awareness. As this occurs we become more alert to the field of sensation we call the body. We become more alive in the body, which further awakens the mind. Noting our states of mind and patterns in the body, we become more conscious of the activity of the mind, not hopping from one thought to the next without knowing what we are thinking. Noting the dreamlike quality of thinking, mindfulness begins to observe the unfolding of thought as much as a process as simply its content. Breaking through compartment after compartment of our little identities, mindfulness settles back to observe the greater whole that was previously frightened into small, poorly lit rooms. When we start to appreciate the mind as much for its process as its content, our bondage to long-imprinted afflictive conditioning lessens, as an invitation to liberation appears.

Mindfulness allows us to not so easily mistake ourselves for the story on the screen in the theater-of-the-mind. The illusion on the screen is consciousness produced in the meeting of awareness (the light in the projector) with the objects-of-awareness (the film's fleeting imagery passing through). As mindfulness develops, there is an increasing capacity to see clearly the passing of one thought after another, seemingly slowing "the film" so it might be seen frame by frame.

Satisfaction with ourselves increases with an appreciation for the process of the passing show.

And when the awareness from which consciousness is created turns toward itself, when consciousness becomes conscious of itself, we see all the way through the superficial mind to the vastness that lies beyond and get a glimpse of pure awareness, that undifferentiated awareness that is indistinguishable from unconditional love.

When we recognize the light behind the shadow play of consciousness, the wisdom eye—the eye of beauty—begins to open.

As our life gratefully unfolds.

When the joy of liberation is what we seek, freeing the spirit from the confines of the long-conditioned mind, from the burden of perfection, from seeking some abstract principle while pretending we are better than we think we are, a liberating awareness is developed that allows for instances such as anxiousness to be observed without the mind contracting around it in identification, and we can see it a bit clearer as *the* anxiety instead of only *my* anxiety. The anxious mind in which the whole world poses a threat reacts *from* anxiety, but when a liberating awareness responds *to* anxiety, even seemingly unworkable states of mind become quite "workable," an achievement instead of a defeat. Calm arises when that which made us feel helpless is liberated by mercy and awareness. As an often fascinating focus reveals, beneath the surface of that which we previously took so personally, we find a seemingly mechanical, even predictable process. And that which seemed to assail us calls forth the heart of mindfulness.

When one quiets in meditation, thoughts ordinarily too faint to perceive come into view. Beneath thought are the subtle contributing factors that forced it to the surface: the tendencies from which it arose. With this deeper seeing we pierce the surface of our dream world. Captive thoughts and feelings are released, opening what was previously unavailable but is now present in the light of a clarifying mercy and mindfulness to the possibility of healing.

I don't know how anybody gets through life, and particularly the difficult times, without meditation or some relationship with some greater context in which our life unfolds. I don't know how we do it without the ground, without the clarity, without the balancing, stabilizing quality—without mercy.

Awakening is the clarification of the mind. It draws the world into a sense of compassion and loving kindness. It is a natural state (some say the *most* natural state), experienced when it's no longer obscured by the hindrances to the deepening spaciousness of the heart. It is the source of the unconditional love that presents itself when we have entered the unconditioned essence of mind.

It is natural for the daily mind to experience the full range of emotions even after the heart's awakening. But compulsive reactivity diminishes. It is not that fear and anger do not still arise but that they stay less long when we allow their natural impermanence to carry them away. When we aspire to clarity, the silhouette of afflictive emotions becomes so obvious against the light that there is less of a tendency to fall back asleep into them. And we are quicker to awaken. Appearing from beneath all our holding to our discomforts and petty annoyances is the clarity of Being. Love is an aspect of that clarity.

Some may imagine that clarity means "a cloudless sky," but clarity is also the quality of clearly noticing the shapes of clouds, their ripples and ever-varying densities, their precise outlines even when passing before the sun, and remembering the light that illuminates them from behind. At night, without the moon of consciousness reflecting the sun of awareness, the clouds continue unobserved.

Clarity is mindfulness plus love. Each sustains the other.

25

A DAY OF SILENCE

THE BUDDHA REFERRED TO IT AS NOBLE SILENCE.

Silence is a pause, a time for reflection. It is one of the oldest forms of healing by turning one's energies inward. It is a mirror for what ails us.

There is something within us—something in the ache at the center of the chest, something in the hard contraction of the belly, something in the tongue pressed defensively against the roof of the mouth, something in the tension in the jaw—that longs for silence. We are constantly talking to ourselves. Because we rarely recognize the fear in our inner boasting, the hope in our distrust, because we don't listen to ourselves any better than we attend to others, we can benefit greatly by quietly settling back and listening with kindness to our interior dialogue. In the gentle and genteel Quaker schools, even kindergarteners find that stopping for a silent pause in the natural bedlam is quite satisfactory.

What might it be like to devote a day to silence? To let the energy that's normally expended in speech be turned inward toward the heart? To let the energy that's usually expended in making yourself understood, in being right, in being someone of merit, go unexpressed? To turn the compulsion toward self-defense, which language is so often used for, into mercy for that painful tendency?

What might it be like to put aside some quiet afternoon to discover what real silence might be? To be quiet enough to hear the racket inside? To let it subside by not turning up its volume into speech? To watch how difficult it is at first to not project the grief of the self-image? To not fill the room with ourselves?

Observing five-minute silences a few times a day can rearrange priorities. Thich Nhat Hanh suggests that we occasionally take three mindful breaths anytime during the day to settle back into our inherent peace. To eat in silence, to walk in silence, to listen to the sounds around us without comment, not reading or watching television for a day, but devoted to the experience of our life that is without distraction. To not divert our eyes from one another because we cannot test the awkward space between us with our usual sonar. To trust exposing ourselves. This is the silence that leads to stillness. It is the stillness that many sages, from Jesus to Ramana Maharshi, have contended is a necessity for our deepest understanding to arise: "Be still and know."

In many spiritual disciplines, particularly in monasteries where the commitment to silence is shared by the community, there is a peace that immediately infuses one upon entry. In meditation centers and in retreat houses, silence becomes the medium of mutual support, and rather than resulting in a feeling of separation, it creates a sense of unity.

A day of silence is particularly powerful when it's shared by friends and loved ones—or even with the visualized presence of one who has passed on. Usually, when there is silence in a room, it denotes a moment of afflictive emotion, of anger or judgment and, though we may be a bit self-conscious to admit it, a touch of paranoia that normally lies hidden beneath our daily autobiographical bulletins to those within hearing range.

I have known people who took a few months' pledge of silence but carried a small chalkboard with them to say what they felt needed saying. Though I always felt the use of a chalkboard was kind of missing the point, I commiserated with those others practicing silence when, at a meditation center, I saw one upon which was scrawled the words "toilet paper" slid under a bathroom door. Noble laughter filled the noble silence.

In silence, time and space are joined. Some moments seem longer than ever; others seem to have passed in a quite unaccustomed flash. We come to know ourselves and the world around us at a whole new level. All the truths are welcomed and invited into the heart of silence. We sit with the saints and the suicidal in the sacred cave of the heart, enveloped in the silence from which all that heals is born.

26

BREAKING THE ISOLATION OF FEAR

FEAR IS THE MEDUSAHEAD OF OUR PERSONALITY: like the mythological ogre, it turns us to stone. Love is the Godhead, the Presence in presence that turns us in care toward each other.

What would it be like to wake up without fear and the aversion it breeds? A day without hiding? A day of opening your heart to your fear? A day in which the fear and the anger do not obscure your heart? A day without compulsive reaction—or even aversion, an almost violent pushing away—to your life? Without habitually turning away from fear or diving nakedly into it? A day without "speaking your mind" when you are dissatisfied, without quite knowing what you are saying?

Turning away from fear is acting on fear, but turning toward it to investigate its inner nature is an act of fearlessness that cultivates courage. *True fearlessness is not the absence of fear but the capacity to stay present to the process without flight or fight.*

Reaction is a mechanical compulsion. Response takes half a breath longer to consider its options. It plays the edge.

Wherever we are playing our edge, there is going to be fear because just beyond our edge is the unknown, in which all growth occurs.

We have experienced the state of fear, big and small, innumerable times, but we always turn away from it, or compulsively express it. We think that acting on fear will dissipate it, but it only reinforces a stronger reaction the next time we experience it. We seldom, if ever, ask ourselves, "What is fear?" We never get inside it to explore its constituent parts, the impersonal, even autonomous flow of the process we take so personally.

States of mind arise and dissolve in the flash of an eye unless we're acting on them, turning a thought into a train of thinking, bidding them to stay. Fear is the basis for anger as well as doubt, dishonesty, distrust, aggression, prejudice, and even, some say, greed and sexual impropriety.

There are so many states arising from fear that we have rarely discerned their original cause, as we can, for instance, with the unfolding of anger: the disappointment of desire stimulates the long-held ordinary grief of fearing we won't get what we want or need, giving rise to frustration, to bewilderment, to pride, to judgment, to aggression, and the recycling of frustration and confusion and a compulsion to react, to "do something about it." We see one emotion dissolve into the next in what is clearly a habitual pattern.

We mistake an intricate process for a single state of mind and, knowing very little of ourselves, think it is simply anger or jealousy or envy, not recognizing the fear and frustration behind it all.

It is fascinating to watch the quality of impatience within fear. It keeps talking faster and faster to convince us to do its bidding. And equally fascinating is to notice how fear is deflated when met by mercy, a quality that fearlessly loves and embraces those parts of us abandoned to fear.

FEAR PROTECTS FEAR
FOR THE BENEFIT OF NOTHING

Gracie was isolated in an obsessive vigilance. She was unable to sit still when her child was home a bit late from school, and was always "waiting for the phone to ring with bad news." She said,

"Both of my parents died in the last three years and, while I feel like now I'm sort of out of the deep fog of that, what I'm left with is a lot of anxiety that some other horrible thing will happen. I torment myself with that fear. I worry a lot about my seven-year-old. Some days I worry about what horrible thing will befall him or somebody else I love."

Gracie's feelings are not paranoia; they are, under the circumstances, a very rational fear. In fact, it's too rational. The mind is given to a kind of Ferris wheel tendency to repeat again and again what it wants most or least.

It is very difficult to completely deflate all our fears, but it is within the realm of possibility, in approaching our life-diminishing fears, to notice our fear of fear.

If your children were afflicted by fearful images, you would take them in your arms and rock them with a lullaby. And so we must begin to treat ourselves like our only child. When I asked the Dalai Lama, considered by many to be a living Buddha, if he ever experienced fear, he replied, "Not only do I experience fear, I experience anxiety." He is a living teaching that to experience something, even anxiety, floating through a boundless heart is very different from feeling it caught in the coils of identification in the constricting mind.

We intensify fear by trying to force it away. It might seem counterintuitive, but the first step in healing fear is accepting it. Acceptance is the opposite of the concentrated form of aversion we call fear. We begin to explore. We examine the pattern fear leaves in the body. We get a sense of the physical state that accompanies the mental state of fear and notice how much easier in afflictive moments it is to stay with the sensations in the body than it is to sustain the heart in the midst of mental turmoil.

When fear faces us dead-on, we learn the power of softening around hard images, literally softening the belly each time it hardens to difficult feelings or thoughts. Instead of pushing away our difficult moments, we soften to them, allowing those moments a wider pasture and meeting them with clarity and compassion.

Working with fear is the key to opening the heart, to keep us accessible to the birthright of our spirit. To stay open to fear, not to numb or close off or lash out, but settling back to watch our body patterns; staying soft, we see how fear conjures so many afflictive emotions.

If all we want is to feel "safe," then that very fear-based desire will leave us forever feeling unsafe. Building confidence in our capacity not to close around fear and thus not become afraid comes slowly. It's not like we will have gone completely beyond fear. It is only fear that wishes to do so. There will still be times when fears as deep as our survival genes will arise. But we will no longer be living a "fearful life."

The deeper our "negative attachment"—that is, our long-conditioned identity with fear as who we are—the greater our inability to let go of our fear of fear, the more cut off we are from the Great Desire to know ourselves, the will toward self-investigation, and the less depth will be allowed to our love. Of course, investigating fear enough to discern its body pattern or explore its interaction with other states of mind always seems easier on paper than it is when we are actually in the dark forest of our fears and are asked to let go of our weapons of self-defense. We have been instilled with the belief that fear will protect us, though some of our fears are imprinted in our genes, originating in prehistory when saber-toothed cats roamed our fitful dreams and death lurked in every shadow.

Indeed, much of what has threatened us has become extinct in our long evolutionary past or in our recent-past childhood. Fear is a product of memory. What we were told, for our own safety as children to protect ourselves from "the friendly stranger" offering candy, can become a misplaced life-diminishing fear of all strangers in adulthood, which keeps us anxious in social situations and unable to connect with new friends and lovers. Most of our fears are transmitted to us in childhood and can take a lifetime to detach from.

LIKE EINSTEINS
OF OURSELVES

When the investigation of the fearful urges, which give rise to so much unloving behavior, becomes a prime directive in our lives, there is an intensification of our life force.

When our "genius for self-discovery" is engaged, we become like "Einsteins of ourselves." Like Einstein, we discover that it is not from the old ways of fearful thinking that our deepest insights arise but from intuition and inspiration, the whispers from the inner reaches of the life force. In formulating $E = MC^2$, Einstein proposed we are made of light. He knew in his heart that the world is created in the wake of the forward gravity of consciousness, that we are created of evolution and insight. He longed for us to catch up to ourselves, to experience the great insights from which a peaceful future may be born.

When our genius for self-discovery continues to investigate how so many of our foul and peevish moods, our anger, doubt, judgment and grasping, our afflictive attitudes, are born of fear, we recognize perhaps the most seductive states that need to be understood to undertake a "spiritual career" or even hobby. Fear is associated with a host of unskillful reactions such as restlessness, which makes it difficult to stay with meditation or keep our knees from unbending in prayer.

Investigating the closed mind (fear and resistance) with an open heart (willingness and clarity) brings forth peace. And quite to our delight we notice that when our old nemeses, fear and anger, are in the mind we are less angry than fascinated. Watching its process mechanically unfold, the observer is less likely to become lost in the observed, able to apply the techniques of softening and mindfulness that leave one with a feeling of accomplishment and even satisfaction, encouraged and capable of a healing love.

When Gandhi was asked about his "passive resistance," he said there was nothing passive about his resistance; it was just nonviolent. This is how the dissatisfaction in which anger is rooted turns into something quite remarkable. Because we have been practicing meeting fear with acceptance, softening around its body pattern and mindset, creating a sense of workability, what we feel is quite the opposite of the powerlessness when we cramp down on fear. When personal dissatisfaction begins to convert into a disappointment with the unkind treatment of others, it turns the heart toward service.

When we start to convert the belly contracted in fear into the outflowing heart of service, when our frustration with the state of the world starts not to separate us into anxious little bundles but connect us into a community of compassion, how different the world we live in, and most certainly the world that lives within us, might be.

Olivia, who long felt separated from the world until she found she felt most comfortable when her love was greater than her fear and she was able to comfort others, looked up from beside the bed of a dying AIDS patient to say,

"I broke my isolation with service work. The first best thing you can do for learning to let go of your fear and love yourself is to do service work.

"I came from a household like so many whose parents had been exposed to dire circumstances earlier in life. It was a house of cold fear that the past might somehow overtake them once again and this time they might not survive. It was a house in which there was no

crying, no emotion, no touching allowed. We never ate together because it might lead to conversation. It was like living in a rooming
house where people just came and went without much to-do. I became stone-faced; in fact, 'Stone Face' became my nickname.

"And I was great at it. But I thought I'd never be able to cry, I'd
never be able to really feel what others seem to feel. So right after
I got out of the house, I started doing service work to find a place,
anyplace, where I might connect.

"A few years down a very rocky road, I discovered the practice
of loving kindness and began to try it a little, but this wonderful-
sounding loving kindness seemed so distant from myself, I had to
write "love yourself" on a piece of paper just so I could get a sense
what that meant—to love myself. What did that mean? No one
loved me. How could anyone love somebody so barren and cold
and dead-ended?

"I just kept repeating it to myself, saying, 'May you be free. May
you come to love yourself.' And the mind would judge and judge,
but I did it anyway. I had tried suicide and every drug that came my
way, so, what else was there to do but meditate and pray? You either die or you try something new. And every day I read a few more
pages of one of those remarkable Buddhist teachers' great words.
Words that told me there was no one more deserving of love than
myself. He spoke into my heart with those loving words I always

wanted to hear. He told me to take myself into my heart as if I were my only child.

"And I began to forgive myself and the world. I had felt nothing for years. But then, little by little I started to feel something. I felt fear, then love, deeper than I ever could have imagined.

"I got into a service team then. It's really wonderful when two people work as hospice workers or caregivers. We worked together and even began to sing to the patients together. Sometimes the love would get so thick I would nearly swoon."

The way out of icy fear is through self-forgiveness and through uncovering the well of service to all sentient beings.

It is said that the greatest service we can do for another is to remind them of their true nature. Everything else is paltry by comparison. You might ease their pain, but you won't ease the cause of their pain until they learn that. But, a great teacher added, "in the meantime feed everyone, serve everyone, and remember God."

First we serve, then we become service. It is a lot like prayer: First you pray, but eventually your life becomes the prayer. First you sing, then you become the song. As Gandhi said, "My life is my message."

True service is the art of returning everything to its source, of holding nothing separate from the heart, of acting in a way that is beneficial to all involved.

From moments of empathy, the heart's imperative to relieve suffering becomes unmistakable. Nurtured by an increasing sense of being part of the greater community, the expanded family of the heart, service naturally evolves.

Take some time to reflect on what might change if your frustrated anger were rerouted in meditations, prayers, and actions for the well-being of others. What if you included even the people you felt acted inappropriately from "a heart which could not yet see," to help relieve the suffering that caused them to make others suffer? Imagine if your frustrated anger were channeled through the ready heart to feed the hungry, to aid the wounded, to sit with the dying, to meet your fear with mercy. Imagine how your small world might expand. Einstein knew.

27

FORGIVENESS

UNATTENDED SORROW RESONATES WITH THE LONG-TERM GRIEF OF UNFINISHED BUSINESS.

Forgiveness finishes that unfinished business.

As compassion forgives us for being in so much pain, forgiveness decomposes the armoring over the heart.

It would be unkind to override the ragged psyche by going too quickly to the forgiveness practice before it has had the opportunity to directly address, to thoroughly investigate, the anger, judgment, and shame of the afflictive states of mind that block and limit entrance into the easy-minded quality of the heart.

With everything brought to a boil in the crucible of unattended sorrow, we see the causes of our suffering frothing at the surface. We also sense what cools the bitter broth.

And we begin to forgive. We may, for instance, focus our forgiveness on the various densities of our sense of being abandoned. Going beyond the separatist mind to the collaborative heart, we forgive the loved one for leaving us, and forgive ourselves for the surprising anger that may arise uninvited.

The first thing some people do is forgive God, while others leave that to the last. We begin to forgive the past and all those ghosts, both living and dead, that still remain unforgiven. By imagining ourselves being touched by their love and their wish for our well-being, we can let the ghost of ourselves be forgiven as well.

We must test everything in our heart. See for yourself what a month of forgiveness might do to the flow of your life. See for yourself what a soft belly, reoccurring throughout a day, does to that day. How much less tired might you be at the end of that day? How much less resistance might there be to act on in a soft belly? How much more love than loss might you find when you tap on the grief point to open the touch point of the heart? When we use a soft belly as a reference point, we don't suppress our feelings. Rather, we give them the space to breathe.

Forgiveness heals what has been left behind.

Sometimes we run our life, our relationships, like a business. Unfinished business becomes the trade-off. "You owe me, I owe you"— if the accounts don't total up, we feel cheated. It doesn't matter if our math is accurate; it's what we feel. "You owe me" is resentment. "I owe you" is guilt. And the longer our interactions go without resolution, the more overdrawn our accounts may become, the red ink in our personal ledgers leaving us feeling bankrupt and bereft.

We may think forgiveness isn't necessary, or that it might be seen as a sign of failure if we forgive. But even the best of relationships among family members, friends, and lovers, because of everyone's subtly different desire systems, the matrix of wants and needs that underlie the personality, may well have some slight unfinished business—that is, forgiveness—that needs tending to. Life is a relationship; openness and kindness keep it dynamic. Forgiveness keeps our life current.

Nikka, bent under the weight of unattended resentment, said,

"My fiancé was killed in a plane crash, and I closed down to love. I said I'd never marry. And I never did. It took twenty years for me to forgive him for abandoning me.

"I felt like an old woman by the time I was forty. I had to forgive him. I wore myself out with anger and repression. But then one day I had altogether enough of prolonging the past and keeping my life at arm's length.

"I took his picture off the mantle and sat him down in a chair and told him I forgave him. And I swear I could hear him forgive me. I said what I needed to say. I heard what I needed to hear. The forgiveness happened and I released him. I was held in bondage with him in unforgiveness. I felt release. I'm free to be married now. Who knows what will happen? I'm not looking, but at least I'm free. Alleluia!"

As we gradually begin the forgiveness practice, we are not forgiving the action but rather the actor. We are not condoning something such as cruelty, for example; we're forgiving someone—the abuser, the forgetful, the insensitive, or even ourselves—whose heart, as the revered Buddhist monk Thich Nhat Hanh points out, "could not yet see."

For instance, we can forgive someone who stole from us, but we're not excusing stealing per se. By practicing forgiveness we are not encouraging or approving of oppressive or injurious action. But we may, after considerable processing of emotion, forgive someone, even ourselves, whose heart was so obstructed, so unable to see beyond its sorrow, that we caused injury to another.

◦——

These techniques, applied with a willingness to heal and a respect for your pain, can offer some of the keys to the freedom from emotional duress you are looking for. This is how the healing practice is done:

Bring to mind a person with whom you are angry.

And, just as an experiment in truth, invite this person, whom you feel has done you wrong, into your heart for a moment. Imagine their presence, see them standing there, note closely what you feel in their proximity. What happens when you turn toward, instead of away from, that person with whom you have unfinished business?

Notice the feelings that come up and how they inhibit your ability to turn the tide: fear, judgment, guilt, anger. Let these feelings come and go.

Now, in your mind, face this person and tell them that you forgive them. "I forgive you for whatever you may have done in the past which caused me pain—through your words, through your actions, even through your thoughts. However you caused me pain, intentionally or unintentionally, I forgive you."

Notice how just the heart speech of "I forgive you" to that person, even if it does not yet have much momentum, nonetheless softens the defenses, as it at least contemplates the possibility of forgiveness.

How does it feel when you begin to forgive others so as to have more room for yourself in your heart?

It's so painful to put someone out of our heart. It deadens so many parts of ourselves. Have mercy on yourself—forgive them.

Have mercy on yourself by having mercy on them. Forgive them. Allow them to be touched by the possibility of your forgiveness. Let them into your heart. Forgive them for the moments in which their hearts could not yet see.

Forgive just as you wish to be forgiven. Forgive just as you perhaps wish someone who has put you out of their heart would let you back in. In your heart speech, you might say to them, "I ask for your forgiveness for whatever I may have done that caused you pain, intentionally or unintentionally. Whatever I may have said or done that caused you pain, I ask that you forgive me."

And, just as a continuation of this experiment in healing, imagine yourself being invited back into their heart and feel their mercy. Allow yourself to be forgiven. Let yourself be touched by the possibility of their forgiveness. In your heart, send them gratitude and be open to their forgiveness.

Then, turning toward yourself in your heart, say "I forgive you" to yourself. At first you might say this with a difficulty that defies the heart of mercy, but say it again: "I forgive you."

How long can you stand this self-judgment, this fear of yourself? What happens when you forgive yourself?

If your mind, in mercilessness, says that it's self-indulgent to forgive oneself, recognize this unkind, unhealed mind that's so angry and so pained.

Let it in. Breathe that forgiveness through the grief point directly into the touch point of the heart. Each breath draws forgiveness from the well of your deepest nature.

Turning toward yourself with forgiveness in your heart, call yourself by your own first name and say "I forgive you" to yourself and feel your heart filling with mercy.

We are part of the plight and healing of all humankind. Just as we wish to be free, so do all beings. Let concern for their well-being radiate outward to all who also want only to be free from pain.

And in your heart-speech, say to those in your life, in your memory, "May you be free from suffering. May you be at peace."

Let your mercy, let your forgiveness and your heart's sweet success at its willingness to be forgiven, fill the mind and the world with loving kindness.

Let this sense of merciful connection with yourself keep expanding to include all those who also seek liberation from suffering until the whole world floats like a bubble in the ocean of compassion that is your heart. Let your mercy, your forgiveness, your loving kindness embrace this suffering planet.

And listen in your heart to the voice of innumerable hearts rising in chorus: "May all beings everywhere be free from suffering. May all beings be at peace."

Many people may notice they have taken the same person for both aspects of the forgiveness practice: forgiving someone and alternately asking them for forgiveness as well.

Stella, a pained example of conflicting feelings of resentment and duty, said of attending to her once-abusive dying father,

"I didn't do something for my dad that I should have when he was dying. I wasn't there with him. I should have been there. He died alone."

We are so conditioned to feel guilty that we are often loath to admit any anger toward the person we feel we have let down. We cannot expect the mind to be rational under such circumstances. Having hurt someone whom we feel hurt us, the vertigo of blame and shame spins out. We try to bury what we consider an aberration, but the difficulty in forgiving oneself persists. Not realizing, odd as it sounds, that it is not until we forgive that other person that we will be able to forgive ourselves.

It may be that you have to forgive the person you most think you want forgiveness from. When you do that, you will then be able to turn openhearted toward yourself.

Thirty years ago, when I was working with the men on death row in various prisons, I met a few whose crimes were so abhorrent to themselves that they petitioned to be executed. Mostly they were people who had been profoundly under the influence of very hard drugs, the long-lasting effects of which gradually subsided.

One fellow said it took years before he fully realized what he had done, and where he was and would be until they took him to the gas chamber. He said spiritual practice helped drag him from his morass, but there were nights when he would tear his own heart out if he could. He insisted they just kill him for his ever-unredeemable actions of the past. But the law, adjacent to the one that condemned him to die, would not let him throw his life away without due process. One fellow even fasted "unto death," only to eventually be force-fed so as to be strong enough to be executed. But no one would have been quicker to say they deserved to die than themselves.

Kenneth, though an extreme example, speaking for a part of us all too easily broken, asked me:

"My grief is not from losing anyone but myself. I am a diagnosed schizophrenic. And in a weird sense I'm glad I'm a schizophrenic because it would be just awful if that was me who did all that. Before I got on this regimen of medication I did a lot of bad things, and now I'm having a very hard time trying to forgive myself. Will I ever be able to forgive myself for what I have done?"

In the process of gradually opening to the pain of having pushed ourselves out of our heart, we may engage ourselves with heart speech to draw the mind into the heart. Turning to ourselves, we may say something like, "With all the pain you were in, how can you not send mercy into that poor lost soul you were, who now has rediscovered his heart and weeps in compassion for whatever torment he might have caused?"

When those inmates began a laborious forgiveness practice, they said they were glad they were going to be alive long enough to contemplate what mercy might mean.

Many years ago, during a very difficult time in my life, sitting very alone by a pond in a redwood forest and practicing, almost as a last resort, a forgiveness meditation, the practice disappeared and only the quality of forgiveness remained. It was pure grace! And in my mind, a voice whispered that I was forgiven for any misdeeds I had ever done. I resisted being forgiven, saying, "Yes, but . . . but that's not possible. There has been so much!" To which the heart responded, "You are completely forgiven; it is all done. If you want to pick it up again that is up to you, but it is all yours from now on!"

How difficult it was to accept the benediction of forgiveness. But if you can forgive yourself you can forgive anyone. And how much it helped me forgive others. If I was going to let myself back into my heart, I knew I had to bring those, too, whom I had denied entrance. I am still working on its subtleties, but forgiveness has within it the miraculous possibility of a whole, more authentic, life.

28

A DAY OF FORGIVENESS

WHAT WOULD IT BE LIKE TO WAKE ON A DAY FILLED WITH FORGIVENESS, a day without anger or remorse?

A day in which we meet with respect all those who have crossed our path. To peer through the shadows that people cast and see their hearts behind, even on occasion "a heart which cannot yet see," just as we at times cannot see from our true heart.

A day of making amends to others by touching those around us with a bit of the forgiveness we wish for ourselves. A day of true heart, treating others as we wish to be treated. Remembering that they, too, no matter how difficult it may be to perceive at times, lament not waking to a day in a healing life.

A day when we remember that to forgive others opens the door to self-forgiveness.

Part of our birth into a life of love is to allow ourselves out of hiding.

Forgiveness allows an unimagined kindness to seep into the lowest sense of self. Judging ourselves, we judge others. Self-forgiveness is not self-indulgent but rather a service to the world, a means of opening our life, perhaps as a benefit to others.

If there were some magic "open sesame" for the heart, it would make it all so much easier. Yet oddly enough, the true magic begins when we, quite to our amazement, discover that it is attachment to our suffering, identifying with it as all we are, that is one of the greatest hindrances to expanding beyond our seeming smallness into the enormity of our true heart.

Perhaps we were absent from our third-grade compassion class when they taught about taking ourselves into our heart. Or maybe we were off reading the Sunday comics, which promised that Santa Claus or Captain Karma would come to the rescue if we were good enough. And when they didn't show up it just reinforced our feelings of "not enoughness."

As I have previously written, when an early teacher first said, "Be kind to yourself," my knees began to buckle and I had to sit down. It had never occurred to me before.

What would it be like to wake to a day of mindful forgiveness rather than anger and resentfulness? What would it be like to not get seduced into the mind-chatter that tries to convince us that anger is noble? What would it be like to instead remember that each state of mind has its own unique pattern in the body and examine that emotional imprint in the body, relating *to* it instead of *from* it? Loosening identification with the states of mind, even at times able to let those such as anger or self-pity pass through the mind without closing around it, without becoming angry or pitiful.

Just as clarity brings with it a loving sense of openness in the body and the mind, anger and fear, in their turn, close the mind, tighten the jaw and belly, and leave little room for anything else. Cultivating awareness of the roadblocks to the heart and the hindrances to happiness clears the path forward.

As an experiment in openness, during the course of the day reflect on what the word "forgiveness" might mean as various people come to mind, some invited, some lurking just offstage, waiting for the opportunity to make their case. As you notice their presence in the mind, touch them with forgiveness. Even the loved ones you imagine need no such greeting. Notice if loved ones resist being forgiven or even take umbrage at the suggestion. Emotions are not as rational as all that. Simply say to them, "I forgive you," and watch the mind's response. Note whatever unexpected unfinished business begins its spin.

Note whatever friends, coworkers, family, or old flames come to mind. And don't be surprised at what occurs when you say, "I forgive you." A portion of the mind is often hiding in the shadows.

It would be ideal if we could just let go of afflictive states, but the considerable momentum of our identification with these feelings is not so easily dissuaded. Sometimes, before we can just be mindful of them and enter them with a liberating awareness, we must clear the way with certain skillful means. We need to meet our merciless judgment of ourselves and others with mercy. Just as softening the belly initiates a letting go in the mind and body that can be felt in the heart, so forgiveness softens the holding in the mind that can be felt in the letting go of the hardness in the belly.

The practice is not to submerge anger or guilt but to bring it to the surface so it is accessible to healing. We will no longer be surprised by them or be unable to meet them with mercy and even a sense of humor that the mind seems to have a mind of its own.

Of course the heart closes at times, but even though it may at times seem hopeless we are never really helpless. Forgiveness is a powerful tool for letting go of our suffering.

If at first forgiveness seems a little awkward, even self-serving when turned toward oneself, it is an indication of how little we have considered the possibility and of how much loving kindness seems a bit foreign.

And for those who feel ill, betrayed by the body, and have exiled a part of themselves, observe how the body swoons when softened and forgiven. It makes sense to open the heart to pain and illness. Every part of us is doing the best it can but is sometimes so isolated, so compartmentalized from the rest that it weakens and falls. This is as true of the mind as the body. There is strength in numbers, which is why so many speak of becoming whole as the path to completion, to liberation.

29

OUR MOST ORDINARY EXISTENTIAL GRIEF

IN BUDDHISM, THE WORD FOR SUFFERING IS "DUKKA." GRIEF IS *DUKKA*, disappointment is *dukka*, loss is *dukka*. *Dukka* is acknowledged as the result of attachment, the holding and/or resistance to the contents of the moment. When what we want does not come, or when what we love departs, we experience *dukka*. But when the student asks, "If *dukka* is personal pain, what then do you call that inborn dissatisfaction some call 'existential angst,' arising from inherent desire, the universal grief at a sense of incompleteness?" the teacher smiles the smile that acknowledges this terrible/wonderful world and simply says, "*Dukka dukka!*"

Unattended sorrow, though rife with the unresolved grief of our previous losses, goes deeper than any pain we can name. It is the delayed stress syndrome of our birth. It extends all the way to our inborn fear and unwillingness to be fully born, a fear that has been there for as long as we can remember.

Most people define grief as that which arises when they have a major loss, which is often a loss due to death. That's one kind of grief. But there is also our persistent existential grief, a congenital dissatisfaction, the universal mourning at a sense of unwholeness, the infinite insecurity of an unpredictable world.

The existential grief that is the "living angst" reaches all the way from the unavoidable losses of a lifetime to the terror of not *being*. It's the dread of the unknown, perhaps the same fear that most people awake with each morning, just below the level of awareness.

It is our ordinary grief that circles like a hungry ghost just beneath our constant mind-chatter and creates the emotional gravity that often feels like it is pulling us down as we struggle to keep our head above the choppy surface. It is the shadow of our original sorrow that feigns sanity, bargaining with a seemingly unreachable pain.

At one time, many psychoanalysts thought that our suffering principally arose from the unattended sorrow of general childhood and birth trauma. They were not wrong, only a bit superficial. Because more than our merciful attention to the loose ends of personal loss or the wounds of the past is required for a liberating awareness to penetrate to the bottom of what is troubling us.

We have to contend with the intrinsic grief that composes part of the superstructure of the mind built for suffering as well as grace. We need to find a place in the heart for the innate tendency toward pleasure and the aversion to pain that causes us to back away from pain and bury what is troubling us, to live as close to the surface as possible, as superficially as life will support. A nagging grief that keeps us seldom wholly present nor ever quite at home. With our fear of our own darkness unsettling the mind, clinging to what we want and condemning all else, we seek a name, a diagnosis, for our anxiety. We compartmentalize our lives, breaking ourselves into tiny pieces, some parts rewarded, some hiding terrified in the corner. Seeming to ourselves almost too fragmented for the possibility of reassembly, we keep our gifts in one end of our spectrum and the unique cross each seems destined to carry at the other end, so that love rarely connects with our pain. The frailties of our mind and body are seldom immersed in our capacity to soften, allowed to float in the ocean of mercy. And the personality we have each been dealt, frail at one level or another, is infrequently reminded by the heart of the boundlessness of our essential nature.

The seeds of sorrow lie in the very formation and mechanics of our mind. Some have been so subtle but so influential that they have been a guiding voice, a predilection for pretense, an inclination to boast and hide, and a tendency to judge that is fed by a frightened readiness to build walls and establish barriers, which narrows our vision and causes us to see the world and those that inhabit it as "other." And inborn, too, in dynamic conflict with this imagined "other," is a need for affection so great that many people eventually find themselves difficult to love.

We imagine that grief will be overwhelmingly obvious, but in fact our grief is as old as our self-image. It is said that whenever we feel insulted, whenever the barricades of the long-constructed concept of self are broached, whenever there is a loss of a sustainable identity, we are, in a sense, exhibiting the unattended sorrow just beneath the surface. Grief is inherent in our self-image. It's tough to find a sunny day sometimes!

Within our ordinary existential grief there is something that clings to suffering yet longs for peace. We are somewhat diminished by the past yet called by the future to find the Undiminishable within.

Of course, when we speak of underlying difficulties, of buried grief, we are still relating to a relatively shallow, though at times intensely painful, level of our greater being. Like the planet we live on, below the mountains and valleys on the surface (which we might analogize to our personality) and the weathering that continues to form and change it (the losses and triumphs), are the deep, hidden caves and long-compressed deposits from arsenic to gold. And below all that is the enormous flowing magma without which the planet would stop growing and freeze. At the center is the stuff the universe is made of.

The road behind us is riddled with potholes. And though we may believe all that is past is past, "the mind has a mind of it own," which sometimes follows a spiral trajectory and must repeatedly pass through the past as it curves off into the future.

◦──

Heinrich, whose loss of his older brother had become entangled, as loss often does, with this "original sorrow," spoke of how much difficulty he had letting go of his sadness.

"I became really attached and identified with my sadness. It gave me lots of perks, a lot of attention and control. I could almost bring a room to a standstill by just staring at the floor.

"I recall that when I was young, I used to carry my sadness like a banner. I imagined I must have been a good person to be so sensitive and sad. I was very good at feeling bad. Then, rereading my journal, I realized what delusional thinking that was. Just another way for me not to deal with my grief, not to get on with it.

"My heart had become cramped closed by holding on to my sadness for so long. I slowly came to realize that to be happy—or, more accurately, at peace—was my duty, my responsibility.

"It was a very liberating moment when I realized I had to give up, surrender, my feelings of inferiority if I was to be of any use to anyone."

It is not just the traumas we have suffered that are the sole cause of our pain but the human condition itself. It is the very nature of our inborn longing for "more."

Hart Crane wrote of "the nihilism of the will," which will have its way. We don't care what we want as much as we do about getting it.

The mind is infinitely insecure because it is capable of imprinting opposing concepts and producing conflicting thoughts and warring states of emotion. We can both like and dislike, be both attracted to and somewhat repulsed by, the same object of our conflicting desires. It is the story of our life. We love getting what we want but are then agitated by the fear of losing it.

A dying friend said, "As I approach now the very end of my life, it feels like there has always been some unease I must settle business with."

Because we have always felt somewhat incomplete, we often think there is one more rite of purification we must perform before we will, so to speak, be allowed through the gates of heaven.

This is a process for us all. It is a rebirth that it seems all must undertake at some time during our lives, and it is most skillfully done before we lie on our deathbed too weak to concentrate.

When we begin to take the opportunity to become more fully alive, to investigate what healings might be available, what options lie beyond our pain in the essence of mind, we begin our long pilgrimage into the heart. We find ourselves torn open to a level of healing, of peacemaking with ourselves and the world, which we seem to have at some level grieved for our whole lives. We enter below what is usually accessible to awareness and see the fear, anger, and distrust, the loving and hating, the arrogance and mercy, the greed and generosity, which give life to our world, and the enormous heart in which there is room for even the integration and healing of our sorrow. And the heart becomes a mirror for the world.

Because we can't elude the pain that's always been there, the light of awareness enters into niches and crevices long since left in shadow. We can't deny ourselves entrance into our heart any longer. When we meet ourselves in mercy, we are more able to love even in difficult times.

What might it be like to awaken with the heart effortlessly open and the mind so clear you can see all the way to its deathless essence? What might it be like to awaken completely free? Free of the prejudice of superiority and conceit of self-degradation? Free of judgment and remorse? Free of the fear and doubt that make us distrust our healing? Free of the boredom of thinking mostly about ourselves? Free of restless thinking while staying open to every creative thought? Free of the hunger for "more" and the thirst for satisfaction? Free of the angst and tyranny of being taught we were less than our spiritual enormity?

30

OVERCOMING
PERFECTION

WE FEAR IMPERFECTION IN MANY WAYS. It is a major compo-
nent of our daily, ordinary grief. As mercy seeps deeper into our
awareness, we can see how our concepts of perfection weigh heavily
on the mind. What we consider imperfection has long haunted our
dreams.

Perfection is relative to our ever-changing idea of what is desirable.
Who we wish to be changes. We haven't wished to be a cowboy or fairy
princess since kindergarten. Even the perception of perfection presumes
a clarity of the judging mind that simply does not exist. The quality of
judgment always has a wobbling, imperfect center.

We attempt to be perfect, perhaps even to become "enlightened," but enlightenment does not perfect the personality, only the point of view. Many sages even disagree about what constitutes the long considered "absolute perfection" of enlightenment.

After forty-five years of meditative observation of myself and others, I have come to believe that there really is no everlasting "enlightenment" or "perfection." I think there is only love and, on occasion, moments of extraordinary clarity that can last seconds, minutes, or even months. But a millisecond of such clarity is enough to give us a new life, allowing us to respond to intermittent waves of unattended sorrow that call for our kind attention from closer to the heart.

My teacher often spoke of the importance of recognizing the difference between theory and practice. He said that when perfection is our theoretical goal, it is less likely we will get liberated. He pointed out that some people, confused by "scriptural perfectionism," get trapped in scriptural translations that call the Buddha "The Perfected One." He said such conceptualizations gave rise to a typically confused grasping at enlightenment: "They keep missing the point and forget that what is sought is not perfection but liberation from confusion and suffering."

Perfection is the nightmare of the self-oriented mind; liberation is the nature of the all-accepting heart. The difference between bondage and freedom can be felt in the space between perfection and liberation. When we liberate ourselves from the insistence on perfection, we see that the perfectionist is often incapable of experiencing those moments of spontaneous perfection.

When we stop seeking to build a perfect mind or body, or a personality to match, and stop judging its absence, we become liberated from the trap of perfection. When we try to find out who we truly are instead of constantly attempting to be different, to, ironically, be better than the place within us where we are already perfect, we get ensnared in others' opinions of us. Meeting ourselves "as is," practicing self-acceptance as a form of compassion and gratitude as a form of appreciation, we begin to find out who we are, who we were, before we were told we could not trust ourselves, our intuition, or our caring heart, as we search for our uninjured and uninjurable essence with mercy and loving kindness.

Instead of getting lost in the ordinary grief that comes from being human, we start to note the same old obstacles to our happiness, mentally labeling them with "Big surprise! Anger again." "Big surprise! Fear again." "Big surprise! Self-interest again." Even "Big surprise! Sorrow again." We attend our sorrow by bringing it into focus, even calling it by name, so that it can no longer hide below our ordinary level of awareness, pulling the strings of our emotions and sometimes surprising us that we act as we do.

When the impatience born of not trusting our natural evolution arises, pushing against time with concepts of perfection, it is useful to remember, as the saying goes, "Spring comes and the grass grows by itself." Patience has many of the qualities that compose the state of loving kindness. We begin to meet with mercy that which we have so often impatiently rejected with judgment.

The process of liberation softens the belly and opens the heart to quiet the mind and expose the grace that is our birthright.

31

THE TEN THOUSAND SORROWS

IT IS SAID THAT "DESIRE IS THE MOTHER OF THE TEN THOUSAND SORROWS."

Many people, when they hear the word "desire," think of sex or perhaps greed. Certainly those are some of the most pronounced manifestations of desire, but they are far from being alone in the influence that desire has over our lives. Impulses, urges, attitudes, preferences, intentions, and much seemingly spontaneous behavior springs compulsively from our desire system—desires sometimes too subtle to readily recognize create our lives, our common interests with others, the attractions and repulsions of relationships, our jobs, and the nature of our politics and spirituality.

Much of our common grief comes from disappointed desire. Disappointment is the natural outcome of not getting what we want and not wanting what we get. Of course, our greatest disappointment is loss. Loss of loved ones, loss of love, loss of safety, loss of trust, loss of faith, loss of meaning, loss of youth, loss of life: loss of what we held precious. The profound disappointments, the unfulfilled expectations that lead not just to "a life of quiet desperation," as Thoreau noted, but to existential disillusionment, a kind of romantic pessimism that's so much in vogue nowadays.

Our desire system, which one teacher said "attaches the steering wheel [intention] to the drive shaft [effort] of our lives [outcome]," makes us continually pursue a particular path or suddenly change directions.

The desire system is the matrix of our wants and needs, of our preferences and predilections that underlie the personality and drive the actions of the individual. It is the "hidden face" behind the construct of the individual personality of such importance, of such influence; it is considered a major constituent of what some refer to as "the karmic bundle," said to survive death and instigate new birth. Its effect on the present is as evident in the taking on of each new incarnation of our changeable life as it is proposed to hold sway over the evolutions after death. From infant to adult (see chapter 34, "The Map of Our Lives") and all the permutations in between, from clinging to this and condemning that moment to moment, from action to action, from intention to intention, our future is created.

Our ordinary, chronic grief includes the cache of disappointments stored over a lifetime from the alternating waves of desire and the losses that follow. Or the mad dash to keep what we have, with impermanence in close pursuit. This sense of losses, some barely noticeable and others too great to dismiss, drop by drop form a rivulet that feeds into the reservoir of grief. It is the ongoing sense of hard-bellied self-protection and an insecurity so ordinary and below everyday awareness that it is often difficult to recognize its origins, much less be willing to acknowledge it.

THE ORDINARY
MECHANICS OF DESIRE

The mind sticks to things. This is attachment. Desire is the motivator of attachment. Though attachment is natural, it nonetheless reduces the vast spaciousness of the mind to the size of a thought, a bubble on which our image is reflected. Hypnotized by our image, we miss the vast awareness in which it is floating.

Desire holds life at arm's length and inspects it for imperfections with the imperfections of the eye; the judging mind grieves throughout the day.

Judgment-laden desire laments where we've been and where we're going. It complains about those we meet along the way, about family and neighbors, coworkers and bosses, friends and lovers, spouses and ex-spouses, and all those it feels have not come up to its standards.

We complain about how we feel, about how we look, about being too cold or being too hot, about things not being as we wish. We complain all day about being alive. We complain all night about death.

The judging mind is dissatisfied desire. It complains from want of something different. It alternately brandishes and is embarrassed by desire. It is constantly in conflict with itself. One moment the mind says, "Have a hot fudge sundae!" and fifteen moments later, as you wipe your mouth, it says, "I wouldn't have done that if I were you!" Battling desires.

We rarely notice the effect of desire until we find ourselves leaning into the refrigerator or, closer to our sorrow, being someone we don't even like in order to get what we want.

But desire is not, as rumor would have it, "bad"; it is just painful. It engenders a feeling of not having, of being incomplete. And then, when we do acquire what we want, it complains about the brevity of satisfaction, how fleeting the satisfied feeling of finally having what we desired is. Or we complain that it is not quite as advertised in the catalog of our desires. It is the ache of wanting and the reality of impermanence in the gut and grief point.

$\backsim$

Everyone has a desire system. Even Jesus and Gandhi had desire, as does the Dalai Lama. At the very least, they desired the welfare of others; at the most, they desired to continue to live and perhaps to evade pain.

Of course the problem is not just desire but our attachment to its continual satisfaction, which turns desire from an object of awareness into an engorgement of consciousness. We are addicted to satisfaction. And in this addiction lies our inherent sorrow because we can never be permanently satisfied.

This is not to say we need to suppress all desire. Instead, we can meet it with a wholehearted appreciation of the moment that does not demand we stop time, but does request that we recognize the first mental image of a desire and be able to discriminate the happiness or suffering of its outcome.

The difficulty is that we stop short at the little satisfactions of little desires and miss the Great Satisfaction of the Great Desire. It is said that to open the heart, to fulfill the potential of the spirit, is the Great Desire, the inherent will toward completion. It leads toward the Great Satisfaction, the very source of satisfaction that is only momentarily glimpsed in the fulfillment of smaller desires.

We want something and try again and again to get hold of it, and then just when it at last comes within our grasp, in that moment of acquiring as burning desire momentarily disappears, we experience a moment of satisfaction. One of the great ironies of the fulfillment of desire is that the experience of satisfaction only arises in the momentary abeyance of desire. The fleeting experience of satisfaction is a glimpse of the source of satisfaction, revealed when desire momentarily abates in its instant of fulfillment. Satisfaction is a glimpse of the luminosity exposed when the clouds of desire briefly part. Our addiction to satisfaction, as frustrating as it may be, is ironically also a manifestation of our longing for wholeness, our desire to experience the greater part of us.

Observing our bittersweet attachment to desire is an act of self-mercy. It gradually increases our enjoyment without leaving a sour aftertaste. Mindfully acting on desire becomes like a window through which we look at the beauty of the moon but in which we can still see our own refection.

Mindfulness of how desire systems play themselves out and what pain they can cause ourselves and others calls the heart forward and affirms the possibility of inhabiting our life kindly and being at times wholeheartedly satisfied. It offers the option of cultivating a merciful inquiry into the nature of the causes of suffering and encourages us to live comfortably, so to speak, inside our life, rather than being victimized by it like a horrified bystander at the scene of an accident.

Desire is a constant, whereas satisfaction is not. Unattended, it can make life seem increasingly unworkable. But becoming responsible to our life, able to respond instead of having compulsively to react, turning kindly toward ourselves with a liberating awareness, can create the central motivation of a life worth living.

32

A DAY
OF SINGING

WHEN THE HEART ACHES, SONG CAN BE SOOTHING. Ondrea
and I have recommended a day of song to many people who, because
of their grief, feel they cannot steady their agitated mind. Singing opens
other areas of the brain; it takes us to other hemispheres. Singing reinforces the spirit and enhances the quality of consciousness we call the
heart.

Sing anything from current rock themes to old love songs, a Sarah
Vaughan ballad or a nursery rhyme. Belt out a show tune or hum a
Bach toccata. Buy an inexpensive karaoke machine and sing your
sorrow and joy. Let it resonate in the waiting heart. And sing, too, with

others by joining a choir, a barbershop quartet, or a cluster of street-corner harmonizers.

Song echoes in the ache between the mind and the heart. It grieves the absence of loved ones and rejoices in the kindnesses we have known.

We find our throat just above our heart. A sound, nearly a moan, seeps from the broken heart and resonates through the throat and out of the body into song. The body is a sounding chamber. As our song deepens, it makes the heart audible, bringing a deeper knowing to the surface so we might hear it for ourselves.

Wishful thinking that things might be otherwise, that loss and death might somehow be controlled, leaves us wanting. But with one breath at a time we can recall the song, hear the flute, smell the rose. With one breath at a time we heal into the heart.

We sing from trust in the process of our healing, not knowing what comes next.

Song spreads from the center of the chest and opens the body. Relief follows the surrender into song.

At first you may be trying to sing well, but that has nothing to do with this healing. This is an exercise in hearing as much as it is in singing. The goal is to participate deeply in the song and to listen deeply, letting aesthetic value judgments disappear into the sound at the center. Listen inside of the sound to hear some of the peace the heart longs for. Let the song sing itself.

We're not simply singing, but listening closely to the song as the sound makes its way through the throat and fills the room with sound and is drawn into the labyrinths behind the ears as it resonates in the skull, forming an auricular circle as the song becomes continually recycled from mouth to ear. It is surround sound for the heart.

33

OUR LIFE IS
"JUST THIS MUCH"

TO BE PRESENT IN THE MOMENT, AWARENESS, LIKE MERCY, accepts the moment "as is." In Buddhism, some teachers say to be free all we have to relate to is "just this much!" holding their thumb and forefinger apart about the length a spark might jump. Just the eternal moment, the living truth, the living present where life is to be lived. The irretrievable past has departed, the unpredictable future is just a dream. Only this moment, whether we call it heaven or hell, is "real." We take time one moment at a time, attending to eternity in fine detail.

Janet, years past her ruined childhood, still scared but slowly finding her way toward some harmony between the healing heart and the war-torn mind, said,

"I spent my early childhood in a concentration camp. I experienced a lot of death and violence.

"There has been a tremendous untalked-about grief in my family. As a result of the camp, my oldest brother is brain-damaged and retarded because of malnutrition. All of us had some kind of physical and psychological pain. It compounded and compounded and compounded.

"Because of these experiences, there was a sense of the pieces not fitting together. And though I can see a bigger picture now, there are still some pieces missing. Though there is now a richness in my life—in the sense that I do not want for anything materially, I have a supportive husband, I have two beautiful sons who are doing well and seem to be reasonably happy people, and I'm doing pretty meaningful work—some pieces do not fit together. At times there is a deep, deep sadness without any particular reason.

"I've been in therapy. I'm a therapist myself. I've worked a lot with forgiveness and self-mercy. And in a larger context I can really see that so far, what this whole thing has done for me has made it possible for me to be understanding and compassionate with my patients. I don't think I'm that way with myself a whole lot yet; sometimes I plunge back into something from the past.

"Sometimes it comes from just watching the news. But every once in a while I can just allow myself to go through it, seeing it all as if it were one of my patients, and I feel an empathy, an overflowing kindness, for that person who is myself in such difficulty. And that displaces a lot of pain.

"As freeing as it sometimes is when I open fully to it, there is the fear that if I would really allow it in all the way I would stop functioning. Sometimes I give myself permission to be with it, but I'm not really completely with it. Rather than being with it, I sort of roam around the house restlessly. There's always a little thing on the counter that I can clean up.

"Most of the time I have a bit more understanding of what my feelings are all about, and that helps. I have dealt with some of these things in a way that they are okay. But it just feels that there is some final thing that I need to do and I'm not quite sure what that is."

Now that you've studied your pain and long offered kind therapy to your wounds, and to the wounds of others finding your way into the shared healing of service work, know that there is always one more thing, one more moment to moment you might open into, to enter time and time again that which waits to be embraced by the heart.

Sometimes the burden is just too heavy to pick up all at once. We have to look at the pieces one at a time before we attempt to form a coherent world picture. Sometimes we have to deconstruct it into the discreet particles that have coalesced into this great mass. Sometimes all we can handle, in fact all that needs to be comprehended to be free, is "just this much."

It's difficult sometimes to even convince the mind that mindfulness can clear the path to the waiting heart, much less trust our suffering enough to open to it even a moment at a time.

As I sat "in a Buddhist manner" on my meditation cushion over the course of forty years, with every sorrow and blessing passing through, there were periods when the reservoir of grief spilled over into my body and mind and was almost too much to bear. Self-judgment, feelings of having missed "the moment" when love might have served but fear had predominated and caused injury, and a feeling of abject helplessness on viewing the depth of my suffering set my mind and body ablaze. I could not think my way through it. The more I tried to figure it out and the more I sought old escape routes, the more the fire closed in. The tighter my body became, the more agitated and exasperated my mind. There was nowhere to turn.

But signaling through the flames was the teaching of "just this much." I could withstand a millisecond of terror—one breath at a time of dread or self-hatred—and that was about all I could stand. Mercifully narrowing my focus to just one instant of the unfolding of consciousness at a time, I could gradually stay with it. In such small increments, the seemingly unworkable became somewhat workable. If we're dying of thirst and try to gulp down water, we may choke. But just the tiniest sips at a time can slake what ails us. Life was too big for me to handle, but in just this fraction of time I had room in my heart for my pain.

It is taught by the remarkable Thai Buddhist teacher Ajhan Cha, a teacher of one of my teachers, that if we can stay aware of just this frame of the inner movie, just one flicker at a time of the passing show, we will find what we are looking for.

Victor Frankel and so many other concentration camp survivors spoke of a level of "meaning" that guided life in the camps and was the center of living from the heart: the meaning given to life by love of others and the possibility of a fruitful future. This was not the "hope" that so often is based on fear, but a meaningful trust. That same trust written of by Anne Frank, that despite how absent of soul or how terrifying people can appear, there is so much more to them than that.

In the camps past and present, as in the ten thousand homes lit long into last night's grief, it is as the heart turns toward others that it finds room for its pain—the heart we all share, experiencing the pain common to all.

34

THE MAP
OF OUR LIVES

THOUGH WE MAY HAVE BEEN TOLD WE ARE AND MUST BE A NOUN, in truth we are a restless verb, a process in process, born into tragedy and grace with unimagined potential.

In a life composed of an incalculable number of moments, perhaps only a few dozen plot the course of our lives: a few moments of decision that change everything. The fruition of previous inclinations and intentions, accidents, and seeming coincidences, which dig us deeper or pull us free of the insistence of conditioning, pass for fate; a few scattered mind moments that, for better or for worse, become pivotal turning points in our lives: missed moments, and moments when the winds of love-karma (each act of kindness accumulates to keep open the path to the heart) blessedly filled our sails; moments of discriminating wisdom or poor judgment; and the effect of such judgments on others.

In Judaism, focusing on the minutiae of this phenomenon of life turning on certain events, there is the belief that we are born for a moment when we will be tested, that eternity hinges on a single moment and one never knows when that moment might come—*so keep vigilant!*

The idea of who we are, and what we call "the self," grows in its particulars—expanding into unexplored territory, as full of ghosts and demons, angels and heroes, as any mythological dark forest that must be traversed. In the widely diverse hatch-marked areas on the map of our lives is this notation: "the mirror house of self-discovery."

Tracking the course of our life like some connect-the-dots diagram, we find in the growth of the idea of the self the moment-after-moment opportunity for loss and gain. In the expansion of the idea of who we are, there are a multitude of constituent elements of our ordinary grief: the low-grade grief that pervades our daily dilemma of being "good enough" and all the other moments of not enoughness that so fatigue us. We find the slowly accumulating ordinary grief of our growing pains, our triumphs, and our defeats. With the growth of who we imagine we are, or want to be, comes varying instances of gratification and disappointment. We are always within view of pleasure and pain.

From the day we are born, we communicate without language. And it does not take long before we can recognize and begin to look for ourselves in photographs. Soon it becomes evident that we are not born "a clean slate," as some psychologists posit, but are of differing temperaments, appetites, and modes of expression. As we grow, we create "a story of ourselves," an autobiographical mythos, the mental construct of "I," which we amend over the course of a lifetime. We build our own little boat and paint our name on it.

As the story of ourselves develops, Creation flows through us. We swing from bar to bar on the jungle gym of our lives, reaching for the next bar while still grasping the last.

Our potential for grief and growth changes from moment to moment.

As we pass through the portal of puberty, much of what remains of "the innocence of youth" is left behind, and with that loss we gain a new worldview. Traversing the "angst of adolescence," the personality finds new means of expression. Denial and confusion, courage, and risk-taking broaden our horizons. We feel invincible; only the sudden deaths of friends briefly remind us that we are not. The future comes into view. We explore new worlds. We play hard. We have boat parties.

We pass through the initiation of the high school prom, trying to elude the time-honored tradition of killing ourselves in a drunken high-speed chase of what we hope lies ahead.

In our twenties, magnetized by lust and seduced by romance, we devise broader strategies for getting what we want. We find new paths to follow until another intersects to take us yet closer to further horizons. It is about here on the map that we come to recognize why René Daumal analogizes our life to what he calls "Mount Analogue," demonstrating that we need to be mountaineers of ourselves to reach the peak of what life may have to offer. It is here in the shadow of our psychological and spiritual potential that some who fear going higher may stay at the base camp, where they hope to be more comfortable and believe they are safer; but those who climb gain a perspective that stays with them for a lifetime. In fact, once we've seen above the lowlands, we are never quite lost again and our view of life is forever offered a more spacious option.

Many people, at their thirtieth birthday, lament the passing of youth. In our thirties, half of us wake up shaking, looking for what lies unseen beyond our disappointment. Some of us find what we have been looking for. Some sleep through lost opportunities and paths left untraveled. We note at times that our boat is not quite as fast as it used to be.

After forty, our most repeated complaint is the decrease in short-term memory and long-term considerations. In our late forties, we increasingly find on our plates the consequences of our actions. We begin to focus a bit more on finishing unfinished business. We test the warm waters of forgiveness. We taste the sweet release of letting go and of letting be. We become more human, with all its blessings and pitfalls. Some people feel their flower is wilting at the edges. Some take up gardening. We check our boat for leaks.

At midlife we realize we may have lived more life than we have left. Some people buy a fast car to try to outdistance death; some have a face-lift to deceive time. Others find an unexpected regard for the spirit. New paths are given closer consideration. Vigor diminishes. Medical considerations present themselves. A few friends die.

In our fifties we need to exert ourselves to do things that were once effortless. What most people define as beauty begins to fade; it either settles in our heart or flies out the window. Our youthful romance with death has quite disappeared.

As one woman lamented following a divorce while trying to find a job, "After fifty, people didn't see me anymore." It is very stressful to become invisible. Feelings of abandonment can arise that are as primal as when we were first denied the breast. This condition of "social pariah" relative to aging reinforces our identity as a body, which of course reinforces our fear of death.

Doctors have found that between ages fifty and seventy many people lose about thirty percent of their energy and about an inch in height. Our breath becomes a bit shorter, our sails not quite full, we need to row at times. Shorter and slower, we now learn the waltz. Some at last learn the tango.

In our sixties we either rediscover some of the youthful joy of learning as new interests flourish, or we uncomfortably age. Some find it the best

194

of times, others the worst. Comfort seems reasonable. Many become orphans.

We take five medications a day on average, depending on our genetic inheritance. Some of us need fewer if we have changed our lifestyles, given up some of our favorite foods, exercised when we would rather nest in our depression on the couch, or perhaps meditate, do yoga, and, like many, remain active into our eighties. Some, lost and bewildered, die within a year of retirement.

In our seventies the garden seems more colorful each year. Fewer friends remain. We learn how to be old. We explore the art of aging or suffer a yet greater fear of death. I have heard many people in their seventies say they felt like they were sixteen at heart. I have, however, rarely heard a forty-year-old say they feel younger than they are.

In our eighties we are grateful for another day. We occasionally check the obituaries to see if our name appears. We may be the last of a circle of friends. Music soothes us. Sometimes we weep when we see a loved one. Statistics tell us that ninety percent of the medical expenses for a lifetime are spent in the last year of life.

In our nineties we practice dying. We burn our boat for warmth. We drink wine. We smoke cheroots, eat cookies, and watch cartoons. Our prayers are the simplest and the truest. Death is not an enemy.

Aging can be one insult after another—if we hope to maintain that perfect self-image that so often presented us with discomfort. Unfinished business raises our blood pressure and lowers our self-esteem. Those who felt life was an endless series of rehearsals and job interviews, and had always felt like an unwelcome guest at its table, may find little place to rest. The ghost of their unworthiness begins to haunt the halls of memory. As unattended sorrow burrows deeper, so does depression. Their life seems to trail off behind them.

Without the heart as a refuge, life can become irrelevant. Loathing the fact that sickness, old age, and death are inevitable, we keep looking for a loophole in the Law of Impermanence. The tides gradually erase everything but love and hate.

Or, aging can be the chance of a lifetime.

Less in the world attracts us. Our walks become shorter. The life force begins to recede from the body and settle in the heart. We love what is instead of what might be. Those who have not yet found a path inward may feel hopeless. Crosswinds may threaten to tear our sails. A storm can break the mast. Sometimes the engine sputters.

In the process of aging, our life force gradually withdraws from the peripheries and becomes focused in the heart. For this reason, spiritual work in the later years can often be the most fruitful of one's life. The spirit is more accessible in this great indwelling than perhaps at any other time. Liberation has never been so available.

Father Bede Griffith, a spiritual seeker throughout his remarkable life, said he learned more in the last two years of his life than he did in the first eighty-four.

35

~

WHO ARE WE WHEN WE ARE NOT WHO WE THOUGHT WE WERE?

BY WHAT MEANS DO I KNOW MYSELF?

Who am I when I am no longer a parent because my child died?

Who am I when I am divorced after thirty-seven years?

When my husband died shoveling snow off the driveway?

When my surviving parent has died and, quite beyond earlier consideration, I find myself feeling somewhat orphaned?

When I have cancer or am going blind from diabetes?

When nothing I have known before defines my present experience?
When who I am now is not who I was?

What happens when age or infirmity, loss or injury, depression or self-discovery displays to me that I am not who I thought I was?

What has become of our hard-earned facade when unattended loss overwhelms us, and we become mercilessly ashamed of being in so much pain, weeping in our secret room? When we can find love nowhere in our lives, no map, no mirror for our heart by which to recognize ourselves?

We know ourselves as mothers and fathers, sons and daughters, husbands and wives, teachers and students, politicians and electricians, men and women, et cetera. But what occurs when happenstance no longer allows us to maintain those models by which we recognize and grade ourselves, when our life suddenly changes, whether it is due to the loss of a loved one or financial collapse, whether it is physical or psychological paralysis? Who we see ourselves as being may radically change when our most treasured identity no longer applies.

When people retire and wonder, "If I'm not my job, then who am I?" they are getting close to the reason they were born. They are beginning to inquire into the being behind all their doing and becoming. Indeed, many do not ask themselves the question they were born to ask until the shadows lengthen. But it's never too late. It's never inappropriate to ask, "Who am I?"

"Now that my familial and social responsibilities are completed, now that the identities for which I was praised no longer fill my day, who am I?"

"If I'm not a salesman [no job], or a parent [children long gone], or a model [cultural concepts of beauty], or a pickpocket [arthritis], then who am I? And since I'm asking, I'd like to ask a bit deeper, 'Who am I *really*? And who was I before what I became? And before that?'"

If we listen past all the ramblings and rim shots of the hard-postured self, we can explore deeper and wider to find who it is we really are. And the deeper we go, the less the question is involved with either the "who" or the "I" of "Who am I?" but more a reflection on, and of, endless "amness."

As we explore beyond our accumulated identities, the "who" and the "I," heavier than the whole truth, fall back to earth. And only the *amness* remains, leaving only the unending essence of being, of deathless suchness, to silently respond to the question.

AN UNEXPECTED
CHANGE IN INCARNATION

Cathy, who had "brought many back" through her years of diligent physical therapy, said,

"I was a professional, working with physically challenged children, always priding myself on being intellectual and independent. Then I got a head injury in an automobile accident, which makes me dependent, and ripped my ego right out of my body. For a while it knocked the vowels right out of me. I could not express what I felt. I felt so alone. No one could help. Now I have a difficult time feeling anything, any attachment. I feel numb. I know I'm not my job, my dress-up clothes, or mother or wife, but I just can't feel who I am."

We can keep grabbing back at an old incarnation as parent or child or lover or teacher or soldier, but it's like holding a dream or like grasping at smoke.

Nothing can deprive us of our true nature except our difficulty in letting go of our identity with our suffering as being all we are. If we searched through the canals that form a labyrinth over the surface of the cerebrum, we could hear the loneliest part of ourselves echoing through the canyons: "I suffer, therefore I am!"

We long for identity and will often take on even uncomfortable masks, not to hide our faces, but because we fear we have no true face. Perhaps it's what the "Original Face" Zen masters refer to when they provocatively ask, "What was your face before you were born?" and only *amness* remains!

"I am this" is the essence of our grief; it is our identification, our clinging to the often conflicting contents of our daily sorrow. What we are proud of is being precariously balanced on the wobbly pivot of our ever-susceptible-to-collapse self-image. It is the stuff of tombstones. One moment we're working with physically challenged people, the next moment we are a physically challenged person. Impermanent. All the "thisses" and "thats" that follow "I am" naturally define potential suffering because that's who we insist we are, toes to the edge of the ledge. And when these identities are challenged, life becomes not what we thought it was.

We've lately been hearing of the crime of identity theft when someone pretends to be someone else for personal gain. But what of that within us which feels it has posed as itself for way too long? Sometimes we find it difficult to identify ourselves without our secret suffering.

And as it turns out, despite the fairy tales and law books, getting what we want won't make us happy unless we can freeze the moment. But the openness of the heart, the presence of love somewhere in the system, brings happiness. Indeed, we are never really happy unless our heart is open.

Resistance to not being who we once were is hell. Letting go into something yet to be discovered is heaven—a little scary, but divine.

LOSS OF HEALTH

Whether we are five or fifty-five, illness in ourselves or a loved one can change our self-image and alter the course of our lives.

At first diagnosis we might tend to panic, feeling we have lost control over our lives. We become imbued with a fear that reinforces power-lessness and thickens the skin of the ego.

But no matter what is to come, kindness toward oneself is the best strategy. I have known many people who, having realized that sur-rounding their illness with fear strangles them, have—quite beyond what they ever imagined themselves capable of—begun sending loving kindness into their tumors. There are miracle stories as well as tales of disappointment that followed, but most felt that breaking the bonds of fear and connecting the heart with the disheartened offered an alterna-tive compass to navigate by for the rest of their lives, no matter how long or short that might be.

A woman in one of our workshops spoke of her illness, clarifying what love meant to her and how much more she appreciated life. Quite to everyone's surprise, she said, "Cancer is the gift for the person who has everything."

Illness, like pain, attracts grief. It draws to mind the loss of loved ones and remembrances of things past that were left unfinished and futures that may never come.

Illness can attract every quality of grief from fear to rage, from sadness to doubt to feeling punished. Our ordinary grief is brought into sharp focus. Feelings of "not enoughness" emerge as well as a sense that a "worthwhile life" has perhaps passed us by.

But some people have said that illness was an initiation. Never before had fear brought to the surface so much of that which had lingered so long just below their level of awareness. Never before had they been forced to confront themselves and choose between self-mercy and self-doubt. As my friend Jerry Jampolsky puts it, "Love is letting go of fear."

A patient who had once been a member of a motorcycle gang and had become blind from advanced diabetes put it another way:

"Being so sick just pissed me off! It left me no one else to fight but myself and I couldn't take it. I gave up for the first time in my life and had to let people take care of me. And Goddamn it, I found some love."

We think of illness as a great loss of control, but never has the heart been so called for. Never have other definitions of healing been more worth considering by one approaching the end of their rope. Never have we been so responsible to ourselves.

COMA

The fear most people have of "losing themselves" is nowhere better illustrated than by their fear of an unconscious, or "vegetative," state.

But a coma, as Whitman said about death, "is different than anyone imagines, and luckier." A coma is like no longer being on the ground floor but viewing it from the mezzanine, watching it all from a bit above the fray.

A woman who came out of a coma after some months said she could hear everything going on in the room, including the unskillful medical discussion about "how long she might last" and the family arguments across her inert body about how her belongings should be divided, but she could not respond.

People in comas can hear and often are reachable through heart speech and a meta-rational trust in the depth of our connection as human beings. Many people in comas think they are in a dream. They don't know what's going on. Heart speech may reorient them to work from where they are. Teach them meditation. Thank them for how much they have meant to so many others. Read to them everything from Peter Cottontail to the Dharmapada. Sing and play music.

Though we may be afraid of the dark, our ability to go further even in coma may be predicated on how far we played our edge any ordinary day. How comfortable we are searching for ourselves in our dark mythological interior, how far we were willing to explore to discover the adventures that awaited—all the glory and gnashing of our teeth of any soul-searching heroic odyssey—gives us the fortitude, for stepping off the edge, we do not fall but find ourselves supported by remarkable possibilities.

And one of those possibilities is that we become love-in-action, like that fellow who served as our driver when Ondrea and I were doing a benefit for an AIDS foundation. We remarked on his unflappable navigation of the Los Angeles highway tangle. Noting his unusual equanimity, we asked him what his spiritual practice was. He said that two years before he had been the director of a major medical research team at a well-known hospital, but the progression of his AIDS had caused sufficient mental deterioration for him to have to resign. He said, in answer to our question, "Now all I am good for is loving and driving. My practice, if you will, is love." And there was no doubt from his exceptional gentle emanation that this was wholly so.

36

A DAY
OF COMPASSION

WHAT MIGHT IT BE LIKE TO AWAKEN TO A DAY OF COMPAS-
SION? To brush aside the cobwebs of fear and distrust and give our
heart to the benefit of others? To not see the homeless, the imprisoned,
the battered, even the prostitute as somehow less than ourselves, nor
the landlord, the prison guard, the corporate CEO "whose heart cannot
yet see." What might it be like to awaken to a day filled with the
equality necessary for compassion?

It's a day of random acts of kindness.

If I react to your pain with fear, I react with pity. But when I respond
to your pain with love, I experience compassion. The somewhat over-

simplified truth is that fear, the lineage holder of ignorance, reacts while a liberating awareness, the inheritor of compassion, responds.

Wisdom is insight into the nature of the deepest levels of the mind; compassion is the deepest expression of the nature of the heart. Wisdom and compassion, though harmonic, are not quite the same. To wisdom, everything is clear; confusion is transparent. But compassion sees the density of things, the pain that needs to be attended to. To wisdom, the pains that may occur are all part of the process from which we learn compassion and the way beyond suffering. To compassion, everything we are going through is important and honored with love. Compassion is an active form of wisdom.

As an experiment in compassion, imagine throughout the day that in your sense of presence, of being present, there is a sense of a greater Presence, a feeling that behind the conditioned play of consciousness there exists a love that knows no boundary. Imagine that this Presence sees you with the eyes of infinite loving kindness and that whatever you believed was your "karmic slate" is wiped clean. Imagine that from this very moment you have been forgiven for every insensitive or unkind action you have ever done. How remarkable that feels, how seemingly impossible, and how completely liberating! Imagine yourself seen through those eyes of infinite mercy.

And with those soft eyes look beyond yourself into a world of self-negating suffering and merciless indifference and see the agony so many people are experiencing. Begin to embrace them, to wash their feet and their hands with the golden light that emanates from your heart.

Send blessings to all sentient beings, imagining how the most compassionate heart in the world might do it. In the heart there is the capacity to see as Jesus saw, as Mary saw, as the Buddha saw, as Mother Teresa saw, as the mystical Sufis and Hasidim saw, as the eyes of the great prophets of every faith saw. Know yourself as one of the many who no longer are so much separated by fear as they are joined by an overwhelming care for each other.

Feeling the compassion inherent in loving kindness, let your boundaryless heart flood the world with kind regard. Let its blessing extend to all those too wounded and numb to feel, to all those who call out for the end of suffering. Let it feed the hungry mind of loneliness and despair that populates the world. Let it say, like the Mother of Mercy who is invoked by so many names in so many faiths, to those in need, "My arms are always around you, all you need do is rest your head on my shoulder."

I have been with many people whose collective grief seemed beyond bearing, experiencing the loss that touched on all the losses in the world. But what struck me was that the wider their sense of sorrow, the more noticeable their concern for the well-being of others. What they had imagined to be a withered heart produced an unexpected mercy.

This slow healing process, this moving through fear and loss, expands with the continued opening of the heart.

When we learn to care without attachment to results, to just love for its own sake, we come to realize that our compassion must not exclude anything, even helplessness. Otherwise, we will not be able to keep our heart open in hell.

Helplessness calls us to compassion.

Some therapists, when a patient unexpectedly commits murder or suicide, have spoken to Ondrea and me about giving up the profession. The therapist's sense of helplessness mirrors the state of mind of their anguished patient.

When such an occasion arises we speak of how these teachings in helplessness can sharpen our presence, leaving us with nothing but the unadulterated present moment, where all our guises and disguises are useless and only surrendering into the heart offers any peace. If our compassion isn't built on helplessness, we will quit when the going gets tough. When we are most needed we will leave their bedside. When we're not in control our heart will close.

As we open our heart to the pain we all share, we may experience some sense of wholeness. When our personal sorrow connects with the ten thousand others suffering this same sense of loss at this same moment, it ripples across the shared reservoir of grief, turning it into an ocean of compassion.

37

A DAY AS IF IT WERE OUR LAST

WHAT WOULD IT BE LIKE TO WAKE UP ON THE LAST DAY OF OUR LIFE, with only a few more hours to complete our life? What are we waiting for? What if we lived this day as if it were our last?

Though it appears on any given morning that we're simply sitting at the breakfast table, there lies between the heart and the gut a vortex in which the body waits quietly for death.

On any given day we have death in one hand and denial in the other. It is difficult to acknowledge death when we are rarely fully alive.

And what if this was the day of days, the last day given, and we had no alternative but to drop our body and breathe into eternity?

It would be a day devoted to the immediate present, would it not?

And on this given day, this last day, what did we wake up to?

Did we wake up alert, with our awareness, our life force, focused, noting even if we awoke on the in breath or out breath?

What would it be like to "practice dying," knowing the more aware we are of the present, the closer we are to our inherent undying Presence?

What thoughts, what emotions, live within those last few breaths?

And what if, instead of the last day of life, this was the first day of death? How long might it take to get your bearings? To remember love instead of clinging to fear, to rest in Being? What is found now is found then. The observed is still the observer. To the degree mercy and awareness are your priority now, these will be the handrail by which you climb.

And if we had one last phone call from death, what would it be? What among the givings and takings of a lifetime might seem incomplete (which almost always means still in need of love)? I am speaking not only of the continuation of our evolution, which some faiths insist we will have an opportunity, even an obligation, to resume the next time around, but also of the words unsaid that even now may lay on your tongue and remain there.

Not to use fear as a provocation for practice, but one of the great ongoing activators of our participation in the life force is to remember we have no guarantee we will be around another day.

⌖

"Is there death after life?"

Many of the Great Teachers, many of the minds and hearts I most admire, say we survive death. Indeed, one cannot in many sects be a true Christian, or Buddhist, or Hindu, or Muslim if they do not believe in an existence that continues after the falling away of the body. Though the scenarios may vary widely, there is little disagreement that there is more to life than our fumbling conjecture of the hereafter.

All religions seem to agree that once the body is unable to hold its spirit contents, consciousness expands well beyond what it imagines itself to be.

From my decades of meditation and working with the dying, I have witnessed many remarkable experiences of our deathless nature, which have demonstrated beyond a shadow of a doubt that we survive our death. As Wayne Dyer says, we are not humans on a spiritual journey but rather spirits on a human journey.

Though some say death is just a change in lifestyle, we may know no more about death than that it does not kill us. We may know no more about heaven and hell but the joys and travails of our ordinary day, but we know that opening the heart is, besides its possible ethereal consequences, the appropriate response for this very moment of life.

Nothing may have revealed the mysteries of reincarnation or the onward flight of the spirit, but we do know that if we go to sleep opening our heart we are more likely to waken to a day in a healing life.

Perhaps that's all we need to know to awaken into the moment in which love and a healing awareness is a constant possibility.

Let's just say as grist for our mill that nothing happens after life. What difference would it make? Does it make our essential nature any less worth exploring now? Does it make loving our life's work any less valid? Does it make wisdom and mercy any less valuable? Does it make kindness, right here, right now, any less appropriate?

Sometimes on Sunday morning I talk to the dead with heart speech. My mother and father, patients remembered with love, the dead children of friends. I listen to their lives and contemplate together all the paths we have walked and all the paths we might have taken, how some choices led to grace. How much we have grown from our pain and how much more from love. We speak of happiness and of their beauty.

And we watch together the snow caught in the first rays of the sun breaking over a distant horizon, descending in slow-motion radiance from higher plains.

Today is a good day to still be in the body. It's also a good day to set up a place of remembrance, an altar to loved ones past and present: photos, letters, bits of memories that bring them to the heart.

Bowing to those no longer present in the body, take yourself for a walk.

Take a few hours off from the life that will eventually be reduced to a name and a few dates on your headstone. Take a walk in a cemetery, meditate in the shadow of a mausoleum, lie upon the fresh grass that covers an infant's soft bones. Reflect on impermanence. Reflect on love. Note, passing through phalanxes of headstones, what remains of a long life.

On a recent visit to death and the love that trails behind, to renew the heart and strengthen my resolve, I was walking through an old New England cemetery, where I was drawn to a family grouping of very old grave markers. I could barely make out the oft-repeated eighteenth-century quatrain on one decaying headstone:

Remember friends as you pass by

As you are now so once was I

As I am now so you must be

Prepare yourselves to follow me.

Above grave after grave are inscribed benedictions and wishful thinking, love long expressed and love long unshown.

One new tombstone recalled that forty years before he died he was "Sergeant Infantry, Iwo Jima," as though he was somehow killed long before on the beachhead, acknowledging that he may have remained as a ghost thereafter, as do so many heart-shocked military personnel.

Some headstones begin and end with the same date; others cross centuries. Some say "beloved child" or "dearly missed mate"; some don't have enough room for all the prayers for their well-being. Others only have name, rank, and serial number. Some are full of death, while others connect with life.

Note whatever unfinished business this walk through death brings to mind. What are you waiting for to forgive and let yourself be forgiven? What are you waiting for to breathe directly into the touch-point of the heart, to make peace with life?

Sit beneath a spreading oak, whose roots are fed by innumerable deaths, and bring to mind the bright moments from your life as well as the words delayed too long. And bring to mind your own unmarked graves from life to life, from moment to moment. How often has your life felt like an unmarked grave, and how many are your resurrections?

Some lives last less than a day, some as much as a century. There is no knowing which got closer to what they took birth for in the first place.

And how do we pass our time now or let time pass us by? What now, on this day of dying, is our focus?

Take a day to follow the repeated suggestion of Plato and the Dalai Lama, Mother Teresa, and the Crucifixion, to "practice dying."

Live this day in generosity and grace, pressing to your heart what is most precious.

38

A HEART REVIVED
INTO A NEW LIFE

WE ARE REINCARNATED FROM DAY TO DAY. WE RECEIVE A
FRESH START WITH EACH AWAKENING.

A woman in one of our grief workshops who spoke of having lost
everything, "and particularly my heart," said that when she lost love
she had lost her life. But in time, she felt something stirring beneath the
surface when she read of the suffering of others, especially children.
Quite to her surprise, she found beneath the reservoir of her sorrow so
much love and another life to be lived.

As the heart revives, many people find a new life beneath their
sorrow.

The death of a loved one sometimes marks the end of one incarnation and the beginning of another. Sometimes it is not until we suffer a great loss that we notice all the healing that awaits.

We have so long mistaken ourselves for our fear and sorrow. We may even feel that without our anger and sadness, we would not know who we are. But mercy can give a meaning to our life that the state of meaninglessness cannot imagine.

Ironically, we may find that, as the heart revives, we have seldom lived in a truly genuine manner, in tune with the still small song within, but rather we lived shrunken to our fear.

And it's not always the loss of someone through death or even divorce that may begin a new life-incarnation; a sense of ourselves not being who we were or really are can initiate an incarnation, as well. Finding that no gratification of the imagined self nurtures our authentic being, that no distraction eliminates our deepest sense of bereavement, a feeling that nothing, absolutely nothing, is worth the heart being closed even a moment longer, turns us toward our great longing for wholeness and bids us trust its guidance to take us where we need to go.

We discover our true life, what Joseph Campbell called our "bliss," one day at a time.

The unfolding of a new life may take us through unexplored territory. We become increasingly open to what lies beyond our old imaginings of who we thought we were.

And consider another of the numerous ironies of reviving the heart:

the most openhearted of us, at times, complain that they have never felt so closed in their lives. Because the more open the heart has become, the further it has to go to close and the more closed it can feel.

Even when we don't know quite what lies ahead, we can learn daily from an increasing warmth to trust the process. Options that we gave little thought to present themselves. In a sense, we are never quite ourselves until there is nothing separating us from our inherent heartfulness.

No one can dream our dreams or pray our prayers. But grace is our true nature. The experience of our true grace is awaiting our willingness to go deeper. And when who we really are meets beneath who we think we are, it thrills us and liberates unimagined potential.

We maximize our evolution with inquiry into the nature of the mind and surrender into the heart, with meditation and prayer, singing, service, and exploring our edge with a mercy that reinvigorates the numbed parts of ourselves and brings us back to life—not a perfect life, but one that resides in the heart. Not a life wholly without pain, but one that is free of catatonia, able to move forward, goaded by forgetfulness and remembering, to evolve.

The heart longs to be free. It sings of nothing else.

39

A DAY IN A
HEALING LIFE

WHAT MIGHT IT BE LIKE TO AWAKEN each day into an increasing sense that being loving is even more important than being loved? What would your first thought be? How open would your mind and body be? How soft would your belly be?

How considerable the day would be. How graceful its possibilities. A day of forgiveness and compassion. A day of grounded kindness.

Of course, love is contagious, and the more loving we are the more we are surrounded by love.

To be loving is timeless, but those who are loved are very much a product of time. What a miracle it would be to make this day a day of healing grace. Some say that the practice of being loving is not only the best support for our life but the best preparation for death, leaving no unfinished business behind and no stone unturned toward the sun.

What might it be like to experience a loving that does not depend on getting what we want but on offering what is needed? To watch each day cultivate an expanding a concern for the well-being of everyone we meet? An aspiration to live comfortably within even a sometimes seemingly ill-fitting world? A sense that no matter what comes next, mercy is an option?

What would it be like on a day in a healing life to open your eyes and actually see the beauty around you? To look into a world more beautiful than you ever conceived? To see into a world of possibilities beneath the one your senses have been bouncing off of most your life? To appreciate how light dissipates shadow on the surface of that which has long been taken for granted? To listen to what you have barely heard as it passed in one ear and out the other?

When the heart opens, it opens the Eye of Beauty, a level of mind, which lies just beyond the sad truth that all we see is ourselves, that, as previously noted, the observed is the observer. To see with the Eye of Beauty is to see beyond ourselves.

When the Eye of Beauty opens, it sees the hidden art everywhere, the grand picture in the details. It sees the design of the universe, the whole of physics, in the swirls of a seashell; the constellations within a fleck of mica; the moon at the tip of a leaf in a droplet of water; the sun in a single falling snowflake; the evolution of the species in the high notes of a thrush.

Repositioning our focus, we find the art inside the art of the brushstrokes on the canvas, in the same way we discover the rising of the Himalayas in a rock overhang, the face of the Beloved in a weather-pitted outcropping.

The source of beauty is not in the light but in the luminescence within. Look at the play of Monet's light on the ripples in the petals of a flower, or canyons in furrowed bark echoing all that passes by, the wrinkles that spread like a delta from the corners of aging eyes into a topographic map of a life long-lived.

Look beneath the threadbare preconceptions of what you ordinarily see to what there *is* to be seen. Ordinarily, all that we see is what we have previously seen. We rarely see the flower—we just see *a* flower. It is not the world that is old but the antiquated translation from the eye to the mind, and all that is lost in translation between the thinking what we see and the actually seeing. To observe directly is to live from the heart.

When we see the present in detail, our heavy lids lift to find, beneath our ordinary grief and suffering, a beauty beyond our wildest dreams, the essential beauty of our enormity. We become grateful for the practice of mindfulness and loving kindness toward all sentient beings and even so unlikely a candidate as ourselves.

The Eye of Beauty sees the essential beauty we have sought our whole lives, that of exquisite grace.

40

GRATITUDE

WHAT WOULD IT BE TO AWAKEN TO A DAY DEVOTED TO
GRATITUDE, a day of thankfulness for what was and yet will be?

Gratitude for the love we have experienced and, even more important, for the loving kindness we are capable of generating.

Grateful for this life in which we have been feeling our way toward the truth.

Grateful that gratitude has any meaning for us at all.

Grateful for "just this much" this very instant, this millisecond of awareness in which discovery is possible. Grateful for the ability to recognize that our whole life is to be found in the timelessness of this moment. That though it seems we are compressed by time, caught between the struggles of the past and the somewhat anxious expectations of the future, we discover, when we look into it, the present moment, "the living present," has all the space and opportunity we need.

Grateful for the breath in our body.

Thankful for the food on our morning plate. Acknowledging with gratitude the blessings from the wheat in the fields, the corn on the stalk, the cow in the herd, the grapes on the vine. Grateful for their lives as they pass into ours.

Grateful for friends who remind us of love, as well as for those who teach us about how unloving we can be.

Remembering throughout the day how wishful thinking eludes this precious moment and excludes a world of possibilities. Returning to a sense of gratitude for all we have learned and how precious our opening has become.

Gratitude for the potential of our heart to rise above the stormy surface of the reservoir of grief.

Thankful for the capacity to experience "sympathetic joy," a happiness for the happiness of others. Grateful for our inherent proclivity to love.

Grateful that just as in the cultivation of compassion we may feel the pain of others and an increase in loving kindness, so in the appreciation of life that is gratitude may we begin to feel the joy of others as well.

Grateful for our capacity to be a bit more fully alive each day.

Grateful for the capacity to know ourselves. Gratitude too that there is nothing we know that we could not know on a deeper level.

With gratitude for this journey and the ways toward our deepest healing within each of us. Gratitude that we are able to go beyond what we know into the unknown where all growth occurs.

May all beings be free of suffering, may all beings be at peace.